Contents

Introduction

State management in web applications has become a popular topic in the recent years. Single page applications (SPAs)[1] - that are only delivered once from a web server yet stay interactive on the client - have to establish state management on the client. They have to keep the state consistent in the frontend application without making any more requests to the backend application. They have to give the user an effortless and pleasant experience when using the application. It already starts when opening a popup in your application. It should be possible to open and close it. So someone has to be aware of this state. But who manages this state if it is not the backend application?

jQuery[2] was a popular library before the first SPA solutions, such as Angular, Ember, and Backbone appeared. State management itself wasn't a huge problem in jQuery in the beginning, because the library was most often only used for selective DOM manipulations. You could add animations to your HTML, add or remove DOM nodes or change the style of your HTML programatically. It made web application more enjoyable by making them interactive.

Eventually, the jQuery code, and in general the portion of JavaScript code in contrast to HTML and CSS grew, and people wrote more sophisticated frontend applications. Most of the time, it ended up in a mess of jQuery code where not only state management was a problem, but also general best practices like clean code were missing. There was no solution of a general architecture for these kind of frontend applications and people struggled to keep it maintainable in larger applications.

After a while, single page application (SPA) solutions like Angular, Ember and Backbone emerged to give these unstructured frontend applications a proper architectural framework. The greater part of the SPAs build up on the model-view-controller (MVC) pattern[3] to architect the application. The mentioned frameworks contain everything you would need, from a view layer for displaying HTML in the browser to a model layer for interacting with your backend, to build your sophisticated application. The term SPA was coined, because these applications are only served once from the web server, as a single page, but then operate only on the client-side. They are blobs of HTML linked to JavaScript which contain everything the applications needs to work on the client-side. When navigating to a different page under a different URL, there is no additional server request required to fetch the HTML with JavaScript. SPAs only interact with the backend to pull or push new data from or to it. Thus, the only thing that changes is the state inside the client-side application, because data is read and written to and from the backend and interactions such as popups, filters and modals have to work. But who manages this state to keep the client-side consistent?

Even though these frameworks for SPAs established best practices, patterns and architectures for the first generation of SPAs, state management became a recurring issue for them. When interacting

---

[1]https://en.wikipedia.org/wiki/Single-page_application

[2]https://en.wikipedia.org/wiki/JQuery

[3]https://en.wikipedia.org/wiki/Model-view-controller

with the backend to retrieve new data, it was unclear how to manage the data in a predictable way. When triggering view related elements, such as modals or popups, in the frontend, often there wasn't established best practice to manage these states. Every framework tried to apply their own solution for it. Eventually, people came up with their own best practices and libraries, but it never became a predictable and consistent experience to manage state with clear constraints.

There was one major flaw with these SPA solutions that led to this problem in the first place: As frameworks, they tried to solve too many issues at once. Because they were the first of their species, they hadn't the chance to solve all issues in the world of SPAs. Eventually, they solved these issues in another iteration when other SPA solutions appeared at the scene.

The second generation of SPA solutions, among them libraries like React and Vue, focused only on smaller parts of the application. They focused on the view layer. It was up to the engineer to decide on additional libraries as solutions for specific problems. That's what made React such a powerful library in the first place[4], because everyone could decide to extend their application with libraries that solve specific yet small problems.

Nowadays, a ton of articles and libraries try to solve the issue of state management. It is difficult to find a consistent source of truth to learn state management in modern applications. Even though, solutions like React have their own state management implementation for local state in components, there are more external solutions coming as libraries such as Redux and MobX that establish sophisticated state management.

Still, it lacks one guide to navigate through all these different solutions to make the differences and benefits of state management clear. Quite often, the guides miss the point of teaching the problem first. In addition, instead of showing the minimal approach, they try to fix the problem of state management by using over-engineered approaches. But it can be so much simpler. It only needs one resource to guide through state management in modern applications in a consistent and constructive way. And that's the mission of this book.

If you want to learn something, you have to do it step by step. Trying to solve each atomic problem after the next one. Don't apply everything at once. Understand the problem and solve it. That's my attempt with this book: It doesn't only teach Redux in React, but state management in modern applications. It goes beyond the documentation of state management libraries, but applies the learnings in real world applications in the book.

These are the heroes of the book: Local State (in React), Redux and MobX. It wouldn't have been possible to write the book without the innovators behind these solutions: Dan Abramov[5], Andrew Clark[6] and Michel Weststrate[7]. I guess, I can thank them in the name of the community for their efforts to make state management in modern applications a consistent and enjoyable experience.

---

[4]https://www.robinwieruch.de/reasons-why-i-moved-from-angular-to-react/

[5]https://twitter.com/dan_abramov

[6]https://twitter.com/acdlite

[7]https://twitter.com/mweststrate

About the Author

Robin Wieruch is a german software and web engineer who is dedicated to learn and teach programming in JavaScript. After graduating from university with a masters degree in computer science, he hasn't stopped learning every day on his own. His experiences from the startup world, where he used JavaScript excessively during his professional time and spare time, gave him the opportunity to teach others about these topics.

For a few years, Robin worked closely with a great team of engineers at a company called Small Improvements[8] on a large scale application. The company builds a SaaS product enabling customers to create a feedback culture at their company. Under the hood, the application worked with JavaScript in the frontend and Java in the backend. In the frontend, the first iteration was written in Java with the Wicket Framework and jQuery. When the first generation of SPAs became popular, the company migrated to Angular 1.x for the frontend application. After using Angular for more than 2 years, it became clear that Angular wasn't the best solution to work with state intense applications back in the days. That's why the company made the final jump to React and Redux that has enabled it to operate on a large scale successfully.

During his time in the company, Robin regularly wrote articles about web development on his personal website. He noticed that people would give him great feedback on his articles that allowed him to improve his writing and teaching style. Article after article, Robin grew in his ability to teach others. Whereas the first article was packed with too much stuff that could be quite overwhelming for students, the articles improved over time by focussing and teaching only one subject.

Nowadays, Robin is self-employed to teach others. He finds it a fulfilling activity to see students thrive by giving them clear objectives and a short feedback loop. That's one thing you would learn at a feedback company, wouldn't you? But without coding himself he wouldn't be able to teach things. That's why he invests his remaining time in programming. You can find more information about Robin and ways to support and work with him on his website[9].

---

[8]https://www.small-improvements.com/

[9]https://www.robinwieruch.de/about

Requirements

What are the requirements to read the book? First of all, you should be familiar with the basics of web development. You should know how to use HTML, CSS and JavaScript. Perhaps it makes sense to know the term API[10] too, because you will use APIs in the book. In addition, I encourage you to join the official Slack Group[11] for the book to get help or to help others.

React

The book uses React as library to teach modern state management. It is a perfect choice for demonstrating and learning state management in modern applications. Because React is only a view layer, it is up to you to decide how to deal with the state in your application. The state management layer is exchangeable.

After all, it's not necessary to be a React developer in order to learn about state management in modern applications. If you are developing with another SPA framework, such as Angular, or view layer library, such as Vue, all these things about state management taught in this book can still be applied in your applications. The state management solutions are agnostic to frameworks and libraries.

Still, since the book uses React for the sake of teaching state management in a proper context, if you are not familiar with React or need to have a refresher on the topic, I encourage you to read the precedent book: The Road to learn React[12]. It is for free and should enable everyone to learn React. However, you can decide to pay something to support the project.

Even though the book is for free, people with lacking education have no access to these resources in the first place. They have to be educated in the English language to be enabled to access it. The Road to learn React attempts to support education in the developing world[13] on an occasionally basis, but it is a tough undertaking since the book itself is pay what you want.

In addition, the Road to learn React teaches you to make the transition from JavaScript ES5 to JavaScript ES6. After having read the Road to learn React, you should possess all the knowledge to read this book. It builds up on the React book perfectly.

Editor and Terminal

What about the development environment? You will need a running editor or IDE and terminal (command line tool). You can follow my setup guide[14]. It is adjusted for MacOS users, but you can

---

[10]https://www.robinwieruch.de/what-is-an-api-javascript/

[11]https://slack-the-road-to-learn-react.wieruch.com/

[12]https://www.robinwieruch.de/the-road-to-learn-react/

[13]https://www.robinwieruch.de/giving-back-by-learning-react/

[14]https://www.robinwieruch.de/developer-setup/

find a Windows setup guide for React too. In general, there is a ton of articles out there that will show you how to setup a web development environment in a more elaborated way for your OS.

Optionally, you can use git and GitHub on your own, while conducting the exercises in the book, to keep your projects and the progress in repositories on GitHub. There exists a little guide[15] on how to use these tools. But once again, it is not mandatory for the book and can be overwhelming when learning everything from scratch. So you can skip it if you are a newcomer in web development to focus on the essential parts taught in this book.

Node and NPM

Last but not least, you will need an installation of node and npm[16]. Both are used to manage libraries you will need along the way. In this book, you will install external node packages via npm (node package manager). These node packages can be libraries or whole frameworks.

You can verify your versions of node and npm on the command line. If you don't get any output in the terminal, you need to install node and npm first. These are only my versions during the time writing this book:

Command Line

```
node --version
*v8.2.1
npm --version
*v5.3.0
```

If you read the Road to learn React, you should be familiar with the setup already. The book gives you a short introduction into the npm ecosystem on the command line, too. So if you are not familiar with this, once again you can pick up the Road to learn React book.

---

[15]https://www.robinwieruch.de/git-essential-commands/
[16]https://nodejs.org/en/

FAQ

How to get updates? I have two channels where I share updates about my content. Either you can subscribe to updates by email[17] or follow me on Twitter[18]. Regardless of the channel, my objective is to only share qualitative content. You will never receive any spam. Once you get the update that the book has changed, you can download the new version of it.

Does it use the recent React version? The book always receives an update when the React version got updated. Usually books are outdated pretty soon after their release. Since this book is self-published, I can update it whenever I want.

How to get access to the source code projects and screencasts series? If you have bought one of the extended packages that gives you access to the source code projects, screencast series or any other addon, you should find these on your course dashboard[19]. If you have bought the course somewhere else than on the official Road to React[20] course platform, you need to create an account on the platform, go to the Admin page and reach out to me with one of the email templates. Afterward I can enroll you to the course. If you haven't bought one of the extended packages, you can reach out any time to upgrade your content to access the source code projects and screencast series.

How can I get help while reading the book? The book has a Slack Group[21] for people who are reading the book. You can join the channel to get help or to help others. After all, helping others can internalize your learnings, too. If there is no one out to help you, you can always reach out to me.

Is there any troubleshoot area? If you run into problems, please join the Slack Group. In addition, you could have a look into the open issues on GitHub[22] for the book. Perhaps your problem was already mentioned and you can find the solution for it. If your problem wasn't mentioned, don't hesitate to open a new issue where you can explain your problem, maybe provide a screenshot, and some more details (e.g. book page, node version). After all, I try to ship all fixes in next editions of the book.

What should I do when I cannot afford to pay for the book? If you cannot afford the book but want to learn about the topic, you can reach out to me. It could be that you are still a student or that the book would be too expensive in your country. In addition, I want to support any cause to improve the diversity in our culture of developers. If you belong to a minority or are in an organization that supports diversity, please reach out to me.

Can I help to improve the content? Yes, I would love to hear your feedback. You can simply open an issue on GitHub[23]. These can be improvements technical wise yet also about the written word. I am no native speaker that's why any help is appreciated. You can open pull requests on the GitHub page as well.

---

[17] https://www.getrevue.co/profile/rwieruch

[18] https://twitter.com/rwieruch

[19] https://roadtoreact.com/my-courses

[20] https://roadtoreact.com

[21] https://slack-the-road-to-learn-react.wieruch.com/

[22] https://github.com/rwieruch/taming-the-state-in-react/issues

[23] https://github.com/rwieruch/taming-the-state-in-react

How to support the project? If you believe in the content that I create, you can support me[24]. Furthermore, I would be grateful if you spread the word about this book after you read it and enjoyed reading it. Furthermore, I would love to have you as my Patron on Patreon[25].

Is there a money back guarantee? Yes, there is 100% money back guarantee for two months if you don't think it's a good fit. Please reach out to me to get a refund.

Why does it use React to teach about state? Nowadays, state management is often used in modern applications. These applications are built with solutions like React, Angular and Vue. In order to teach about state management, it makes sense to apply it in a real world context such as React. I picked React, because it has only a slim API and a good learning curve. It is only the view layer with local state management. You can learn about it in one of my other books: the Road to learn React[26]. However, you don't necessarily need to apply your learnings about state management in React. You can apply these learnings in your Angular, Vue or React Native application, too.

What is the ratio between learning Redux and MobX? Even though MobX becomes more of a popular alternative to Redux, the book teaches you more about Redux than MobX. However, in the future I want to extend the content and depending on the popularities adjust the chapters.

What's your motivation behind the book? I want to teach about this topic in a consistent way. You often find material online that doesn't receive any updates or only teaches a small part of a topic. When you learn something new, people struggle to find consistent and up-to-date resources to learn from. I want to give you this consistent and up-to-date learning experience. In addition, I hope I can support minorities with my projects by giving them the content for free or by having other impacts[27]. In addition, in the recent time, I found myself fulfilled when teaching others about programming. It's a meaningful activity for me that I prefer over any other 9 to 5 job at any company. That's why I hope to pursue this path in the future.

Is there a call to action? Yes. I want you to take a moment to think about a person who would be a good match to learn Redux. The person could have shown the interest already, could be in the middle of learning Redux or might not yet be aware about wanting to learn Redux. Reach out to that person and share the book. It would mean a lot to me. The book is intended to be given to others.

---

[24]https://www.robinwieruch.de/about/

[25]https://www.patreon.com/rwieruch

[26]https://www.robinwieruch.de/the-road-to-learn-react/

[27]https://www.robinwieruch.de/giving-back-by-learning-react/

How to read the Book

One thing is certain, no one learned programming by just reading a book. Programming is about hands on experiences. It is about conquering challenges to grow in the long term. So no one learned a programming paradigm, such as functional programming, in the short term. No one learned a concept, such as state management, on a weekend. No one learned yet another library, such as React, over one night. You will learn things only by deliberately practicing them.

In the book, I want to give you these hands on experiences and challenges to grow. The challenges are meant to create a flow experience, a scenario where the challenge meets your skills and tools at hand. Otherwise, you would feel either overwhelmed or bored. If the book accomplishes to keep this balance of challenging you and respecting your level of skill, you might experience a state of flow[28]. Personally I found this insight astonishing when I read about it, so I hope that I can induce it in this book. It would be the perfect outcome.

The book follows the central theme of state management in modern applications. It starts with local state management in a view library (React), points out the problems of it in scaling applications and will lead over to sophisticated state management solutions such as Redux and MobX. While you read the book, you will find code playgrounds that illustrate problems and solutions. I encourage you to play around with these code playgrounds to have a hands on experience. You can even try to apply these code snippets in your own editor and play around with them. But don't worry if it doesn't work out. You will be guided to apply your learnings in your own editor in various chapters. However, don't hesitate to apply the learnings earlier on your own. You will only grow when facing those challenges.

As mentioned, there are guided hands on experiences in the book. There, you will be guided to solve problems by using the techniques you have learned in previous chapters. You will solve these problems in an online editor, that is already prepared, or in your own editor. It should give you the experience of applying your learnings beyond only reading a book. This book aims to go beyond only being reading material. It's supposed to be a practical hands-on guide that let's you apply your learnings in order to deepen your knowledge.

Be aware that the JS BIN[29] online editor, that you are going to use occasionally, will not always provide all functionalities from modern browsers. For instance, you might run into problems when trying to apply JavaScript ES6 and beyond functionalities. That's why the book tries to transition to project in your own editor as soon as possible. There you have full control over your projects and can continue working on the projects even after you read the book.

In addition, make sure to internalize each lesson learned before you continue with the next chapter. The book is written in a way that the learnings build up on each other. Your knowledge around about the taught topics will not only scale horizontally by using different techniques but also vertically by deploying technique on technique. That's why it is important to internalize each learning before your continue to read.

---

[28]https://www.robinwieruch.de/lessons-learned-deep-work-flow/

[29]http://jsbin.com/

The React library is used as view layer library in this book to demonstrate the usage of state management in modern applications. However, fortunately, a view layer is exchangeable. If you are learning state management to apply it to another view layer library, such as Vue or Angular, you can try to substitute React with Vue or Angular on your own. The book doesn't want to dictate the view layer library or framework. If you are brave, you can apply the learnings in your very own application where you want to introduce state management.

Another recommendation is making notes while you read the book. You can write down questions where the book doesn't give you an answer and look them up afterward. Or you can write down your learnings to internalize them. That is how I do it when I read a book. Last but not least, if you write down feedback about the book, you can send me your notes afterward. I am highly interested to improve the book all the time to keep the quality up.

It should be obvious by now that you will have the best outcome of this book by having a laptop on your side. You can join the Slack Group[30] to get help from others or to help others yourself. When having a laptop on your side, you can directly apply your new learnings and confront yourself with the practical oriented chapters. As mentioned before, no one learned something by just reading a book, so keep on practicing your learnings.

---

[30]https://slack-the-road-to-learn-react.wieruch.com/

Local State Management

This chapter will guide you through state management in React without taking any external state management library into account. You will revisit state management in React with only `this.setState()` and `this.state`. It enables you to build medium sized applications without complicating and over-engineering it. It is important to remember this statement: Not every application needs external state management in the first place. I can tell you from experience that many companies out there went all in with React and Redux, only to recognize that they didn't need Redux for their application. It didn't have the complexity to introduce external libraries for it. React's state management would have been sufficient.

By revisiting the topic of local state management in React, you will get to know how to use the local state for React applications which don't need a state management library such as Redux. The chapter guides you through important topics when dealing with state in React: controlled components, unidirectional data flow and asynchronous state. It will teach you all these necessary topics before diving into state management with an external state management library.

After revisiting the local state in React, you will get to know best practices and patterns to scale your state management when using only local state. Even though you are not dependent on external state management solutions yet, you can use a handful of those techniques to scale state management with external libraries, too, which are described later on in this book.

At the end of the chapter, you will get to know the limits of local state management in React. The topic itself is highly discussed in the community as you will learn in one of the final lessons of this chapter. The chapter concludes in the problem of local state management to give you a motivation to dive into one of the external state management solutions.

Definitions

Before we dive into state management, this chapter gives you general definitions and definitions for state managements to build up a common vocabulary for state management for this book. It should help you to follow the book effortlessly when reading it without leaving space for confusion.

Pure Functions

Pure functions is a concept from the functional programming paradigm. It says that a pure function always returns the same output if given the same input. There is no layer in between that could alter the output on the way when the input doesn't change. The layer in between, that could possibly alter the output, is called **side-effect**. Thus, pure functions have no side-effects. Two major benefits of these pure functions are predictability and testability.

Immutability

Immutability is a concept of functional programming, too. It says that a data structure is immutable when it cannot be changed. When there is the need to modify the immutable data structure, for instance an object, you would always return a new object. Rather than altering the object at hand, you would create a new object based on the old object and the modification. The old and new object would have their own instances.

Immutable data structures have the benefit of predictability. For instance, when sharing an object through the whole application, it could lead to bugs when altering the object directly, because every stakeholder has a reference to this potentially altered object. It would be unpredictable what happens when an object changes and a handful of stakeholders, such as UI components, are dependent on this object. In a growing application, it is difficult to oversee the places where the object is currently used by its reference.

Note: The antagonist of immutability is called mutability. It says that an object can be modified.

State

State is a broad word in modern applications. When speaking about **application state**, it could be anything that needs to be stored and be **managed (created, updated, deleted)** in the application. The state can be **remote data** which is fetched from a backend application or **view data** which lives only on the client-side of the application.

I will refer to the former one as **entity state** and to the latter one as **view state**. Entity state is data retrieved from a backend application. It could be a list of authors or the user object describing the user that is currently logged in to the application. View state, on the other hand, doesn't need to be stored in the backend. It is used when you open up a modal or switch a box from preview to edit mode.

When speaking about managing the state, meaning creating, updating and deleting state, it will be coined under the umbrella term of state management. Yet, state management is a much broader topic. While the mentioned actions are low-level operations, almost implementation details, the architecture, best practices and patterns around state management stay abstract. **State management** involves all these topics to keep your application state durable.

The Size of State

State can be an atomic object or one large aggregated object. When speaking about the view state, that only determines whether a popup is open or closed, it is an **atomic state object**. When the whole application state can be derived from one aggregated object, which includes all the atomic state objects, it is called a **global state object**. Often, a global state object implies that it is accessible from everywhere.

The state itself can be differentiated into **local state** and **sophisticated state**. The management of this state is called **local state management** and **sophisticated state management**.

Local State

The naming local state is widely accepted in the web development community. Another term might be **internal component state**. Local state is bound to components or component hierarchies. It lives in the view layer. It is not stored somewhere else outside of this view layer. That's why it is called local state because it is co-located to the component.

In React, the local state is embraced by using `this.state` and `this.setState()`. But it can have a different implementation and usage in other view layer or SPA solutions. The book explains and showcases the local state in React before diving into sophisticated state management with external libraries such as Redux and MobX.

Sophisticated State

I cannot say that it is widely agreed on to call it sophisticated state in the web development community. However, at some point you need a term to distinguish it from local state. That's why I often refer to it as sophisticated state. In other resources, you might find it referred to as **external state**, because it lives outside of the UI components or outside of the view layer.

Most often, sophisticated state is outsourced to libraries that are library or framework agnostic and thus agnostic to the view layer. But most often they provide a bridge to access and modify state from the view layer. When using only local state in a scaling application, you will allocate too much state along your components in the view layer. However, at some point you want to separate view layer and state layer, because the state becomes too complex. That's when sophisticated state comes into play.

Two libraries that are known for managing sophisticated state are called Redux and MobX. Both libraries will be explained, discussed and showcased in this book.

Visibility of State

Since local state is only bound to the component instance, only the component itself is aware of these properties being state. However, the component can share the state to its child components. In React, the child components are unaware of these properties being state. They only receive these properties as props.

On the other hand, sophisticated state is often globally accessible. In theory, the state can be accessed by each component. Often, it is not best practice to give every component access to the global state, thus it is up to the developer to bridge only selected components to the global state object. All other components stay unaware of the state and only receive properties as props to act on them.

Local State in React

The book uses React as view layer for demonstrating the local state in a web application. The following chapter focusses on the local state in React before it dives into sophisticated state management with Redux and MobX. As mentioned, the concept of local state should be known in other SPA solutions, too, and thus be applicable in those solutions.

So, what does local state look like in a React component?

Code Playground

```
import React from 'react';

class Counter extends React.Component {
  constructor(props) {
    super(props);

    this.state = {
      counter: 0
    };
  }

  render() {
    return (
      <div>
        <p>{this.state.counter}</p>
      </div>
    );
  }
}
```

The example shows a `Counter` component that has a `counter` property in the local state object. It is defined with a value of `0` when the component gets instantiated by its constructor. In addition, the `counter` property from the local state object is used in the render method of the component to display its current value.

There is no state manipulation in place yet. Before you start to manipulate your state, you should know that you are never allowed to mutate the state directly: `this.state.counter = 1`. That would be a direct mutation. Instead, you have to use the React component API to change the state explicitly by using the `this.setState()` method. It keeps the state object immutable, because the state object isn't changed but a new modified copy of it is created.

Code Playground

```
import React from 'react';

class Counter extends React.Component {
  constructor(props) {

    ...

    this.onIncrement = this.onIncrement.bind(this);
    this.onDecrement = this.onDecrement.bind(this);
  }

  onIncrement() {
    this.setState({
      counter: this.state.counter + 1
    });
  }

  onDecrement() {
    this.setState({
      counter: this.state.counter - 1
    });
  }

  render() {

    ...

  }
}
```

The class methods can be used in the render() method to trigger the local state changes.

Code Playground

```
import React from 'react';

class Counter extends React.Component {

  ...

  render() {
    return (
      <div>
        <p>{this.state.counter}</p>
        <button type="button" onClick={this.onIncrement}>
```

```
        Increment
      </button>
      <button type="button" onClick={this.onDecrement}>
        Decrement
      </button>
    </div>
  );
  }
}
```

Now, the button onClick handler should invoke the class methods to alter the state by either incrementing or decrementing the counter value. Then, the update functionality with this.setState() is performing a **shallow merge** of objects. What does a shallow merge mean? Imagine you had the following state in your component, two arrays with objects:

Code Playground

```
this.state = {
  authors: [...],
  articles: [...],
};
```

When updating the state only partly, for instance the authors, the other part, in this case the articles, are left intact.

Code Playground

```
this.setState({
  authors: [
    { name: 'Robin', id: '1' }
  ]
});
```

It only updates the authors array with a new array without touching the articles array. That's called a shallow merge. It simplifies the local state management for you so that you don't have to keep an eye on all properties at once in the local state.

Stateful and Stateless Components

Local state can only be used in React ES6 class components. The component becomes a **stateful component** when state is used. Otherwise, it can be called **stateless component** even though it is still a React ES6 class component. This can be the case if you still need to use React's lifecycle methods.

On the other hand, **functional stateless components** have no state, because, as the name implies, they are only functions and thus, they are stateless. They get input as props and return output as JSX. In a stateless component, state can only be passed as props from a parent component. However, the functional stateless component is unaware of the props being state in the parent component. In addition, callback functions can be passed down to the functional stateless component to have an indirect way of altering the state in the parent component again. A functional stateless component for the Counter example could look like the following:

Code Playground

```
import React from 'react';

function CounterPresenter(props) {
  return (
    <div>
      <p>{props.counter}</p>
      <button type="button" onClick={props.onIncrement}>
        Increment
      </button>
      <button type="button" onClick={props.onDecrement}>
        Decrement
      </button>
    </div>
  );
}
```

Now only the props from the parent component would be used in this functional stateless component. The counter prop would be displayed and the two callback functions, onIncrement() and onDecrement() would be used for the buttons. However, the functional stateless component is not aware whether the passed properties are state, props or some other derived properties. The origin of the props doesn't need to be in the parent component after all, it could be somewhere higher up the component tree. The parent component would only pass the properties or derived properties along the way. In addition, the component is unaware of what the callback functions are doing. It doesn't know that these alter the local state of the parent component.

After all, the callback functions in the stateless component would make it possible to alter the state somewhere above in one of the parent components. Once the state was manipulated, the new state flows down as props into the child component again. The new counter prop would be displayed correctly, because the render method of the child component runs again with the incoming changed props.

The example shows how local state can traverse down from one component to the component tree. To make the example with the functional stateless component complete, let's quickly show what a potential parent component, that manages the local state, would look like. It is a React ES6 class component in order to be stateful.

Code Playground

```
import React from 'react';

class CounterContainer extends React.Component {
  constructor(props) {
    super(props);

    this.state = {
      counter: 0
    };

    this.onIncrement = this.onIncrement.bind(this);
    this.onDecrement = this.onDecrement.bind(this);
  }

  onIncrement() {
    this.setState({
      counter: this.state.counter + 1
    });
  }

  onDecrement() {
    this.setState({
      counter: this.state.counter - 1
    });
  }

  render() {
    return <CounterPresenter
      counter={this.state.counter}
      onIncrement={this.onIncrement}
      onDecrement={this.onDecrement}
    />
  }
}
```

It is not by accident that the suffixes in the naming of both Counter components are Container and `Presenter`. It is called the container and presentational component pattern[31]. It is most often applied in React, but could live in other component centred libraries and frameworks, too. If you have never heard about it, I recommend reading the referenced article. It is a widely used pattern, where the container component deals with "How things work" and the presenter component deals with "How things look". In this case, the container component cares about the state while the presenter component only displays the counter value and provides a handful of click handler yet without knowing that these click handlers manipulate the state. Note that the presenter component is called presentational component in the referenced article. I shortened the name from presentational to presenter component for the sake of convenience.

Container components are the ideal candidates to manage state while the presenter components only display it and act on callback functions. You will encounter these container components more often in the book, when dealing with the concepts of higher-order components, that could potentially manage local state, and connected components.

Props vs. State

The previous example made clear that there is a difference between state and props in React. When properties are passed to a child component, whether it is state, props or derived properties, the child component isn't aware of the kind of properties. It sees the incoming properties as props. That's perfect, because the component shouldn't care at all about the kind of properties. It should only make use of them as simple props.

The props come from a parent component. In the parent component these props can be state, props or derived properties. It depends on the parent component, if it manages the properties itself (state), if it gets the properties from a parent component itself (props) or if it derives new properties from the incoming props coming from its parent component along the way (derived properties).

After all, you can't modify props. Props are only properties passed from a parent component to a child component. On the other hand, the local state lives in the component itself. You can access it by using `this.state`, modify it by using `this.setState()`, and pass it down as props to child components.

When one of these objects changes, whether it is the props that come from the parent component or the state in the component, the update lifecycle methods of the component will run. One of these lifecycle methods is the `render()` method that updates your component instance based on the props and state. The correct values will be used and displayed after the update ran in your component.

When you start to use React, it might be difficult to identify props and state. Personally, I like the rules in the official React documentation[32] to identify state and props:

- Are the properties passed from the parent component? If yes, the likelihood is high that they aren't state. Though it is possible to save props as state, there are little use cases. It should be avoided to save props as state. Use them as props as they are.

---

[31]https://medium.com/@dan_abramov/smart-and-dumb-components-7ca2f9a7c7d0

[32]https://reactjs.org/docs/thinking-in-react.html

- Are the properties unchanged over time? If yes, they don't need to be stateful, because they don't get modified.
- Are the properties derivable from local state or props? If yes, you don't need them as state, because you can derive them. If you allocated extra state, the state has to be managed and can get out of sync when you miss to derive the new properties at some point.

Form State

A common use case in applications is to use HTML forms. For instance, you might need to retrieve user information like a name or credit card number or submit a search query to an external API. Forms are used everywhere in web applications.

There are two ways to use forms in React. You can use the ref attribute or local state. It is recommended to use the local state approach, because the ref attribute is reserved for only a few use cases. If you want to read about these use cases when using the ref attribute, I encourage you to read the following article: When to use Ref on a DOM node in React[33].

The following code snippet is a quick demonstration on how form state can be used by using the ref attribute. Afterward, the code snippet will get refactored to use the local state which is the best practice anyway.

Code Playground

```
import React from 'react';

class Search extends React.Component {
  constructor(props) {
    super(props);

    this.onSubmit = this.onSubmit.bind(this);
  }

  onSubmit(event) {
    const { value } = this.input;

    // do something with the search value
    // e.g. propagate it up to the parent component
    this.props.onSearch(value);

    event.preventDefault();
  }

  render() {
```

---

[33]https://www.robinwieruch.de/react-ref-attribute-dom-node/

```
    return (
      <form onSubmit={this.onSubmit}>
        <input
          ref={node => this.input = node}
          type="text"
        />
        <button type="submit">
          Search
        </button>
      </form>
    );
  }
}
```

The value from the input node is retrieved by using the reference to the DOM node. It happens in the onSubmit() method. The reference is created by using the ref attribute in the render() method.

Now let's see how to make use of local state to embrace best practices rather than using the reserved ref attribute.

Code Playground

```
import React from 'react';

class Search extends React.Component {
  constructor(props) {
    super(props);

    this.state = {
      query: ''
    };

    this.onChange = this.onChange.bind(this);
    this.onSubmit = this.onSubmit.bind(this);
  }

  onChange(event) {
    const { value } = event.target;

    this.setState({
      query: value
    });
  }
```

```
onSubmit(event) {
  const { query } = this.state;

  // do something with the search value
  // e.g. propagate it up to the parent component
  this.props.onSearch(query);

  event.preventDefault();
}

render() {
  return (
    <form onSubmit={this.onSubmit}>
      <input
        onChange={this.onChange}
        type="text"
      />
      <button type="submit">
        Search
      </button>
    </form>
  );
}
}
```

You don't need to make use of the ref attribute anymore. You can solve the problem by using local state only. The example demonstrates it with only one input field yet it can be used with multiple input fields, too. You would only need to allocate more properties, one for each input field, in the local state.

Controlled Components

The previous example of using form state with local state has one flaw. It doesn't make use of **controlled components**. Naturally, a HTML input field holds its own state. When you enter a value into the input field, the DOM node knows about the value. That's the native behavior of HTML elements, otherwise they wouldn't work on their own.

However, the value lives in your local state, too. You have it in both, the native DOM node state and local state. But you want to make use of a single source of truth. It is a best practice to overwrite the native DOM node state by using the value attribute on the HTML element and the value from the local state from the React component.

Let's consider the previous example again. The input field had no value attribute assigned. By using the native value attribute and passing the local state as value, you convert an uncontrolled component to a controlled component.

Code Playground

```
import React from 'react';

class Search extends React.Component {

  ...

  render() {
    return (
      <form onSubmit={this.onSubmit}>
        <input
          value={this.state.query}
          onChange={this.onChange}
          type="text"
        />
        <button type="submit">
          Search
        </button>
      </form>
    );
  }
}
```

Now the value comes from the local state as single source of truth. It cannot get out of sync with the native DOM node state. This way, you can provide an initial state for the DOM node state too. Otherwise, try to have an initial local state for the query in your local state, but don't provide the value attribute to the input field. Your state would be out of sync in the beginning, because the input field would be empty even though the local state of the React component says something else.

Unidirectional Data Flow

In the previous example, you experienced a typical unidirectional data flow. The Flux architecture, the underlying architecture for several sophisticated state management solutions such as Redux, coined the term **unidirectional data flow**. You will get to know more about the Flux architecture in a later chapter. But the essence of an unidirectional data flow is embraced by local state in React, too. State in React flows only in one direction. State gets updated by using this.setState() and is displayed due to the render() lifecycle method by accessing this.state. Then again, it can be updated via this.setState() and a component re-renders.

The previous example, where you have used controlled components, shows the perfect loop of the unidirectional data flow. The input field triggers the onChange handler when the input changes. The handler alters the local state. The changed local state triggers an update lifecycle of the component. The update lifecycle runs the render() lifecycle method again. The render() method makes use of the updated state. The state flows back to the input field to make it a controlled component. The loop is closed. A new loop can be triggered by typing something into the input field again.

The unidirectional data flow makes state management predictable and maintainable. The best practice already spread to other state libraries, view layer libraries and SPA solutions. In the previous generation of SPAs, most often other mechanics were used. For instance, in Angular 1.x you would have used two-way data binding in a model-view-controller (MVC) architecture. That means, once you changed the value in the view, let's say in an input field by typing something, the value got changed in the controller. But it worked vice versa, too. Once you had changed the value in the controller programmatically, the view, to be more specific the input field, displayed the new value. You might wonder: What's the problem with this approach? Why is everybody using unidirectional data flow instead of bidirectional data flow now?

Unidirectional vs. Bidirectional Data Flow

React embraces unidirectional data flow. In the past, frameworks like Angular 1.x embraced bidirectional data flow. It was known as two-way data binding. It was one of the reasons that made Angular popular in the first place. But it failed in this particular area, too. Especially, in my opinion, this particular flaw led a lot of people to switch to React. But at this point I don't want to get too opinionated. So why did the bidirectional data flow fail? Why is everyone adopting the unidirectional data flow?

The three advantages in unidirectional data flow over bidirectional data flow are predicability, maintainability and performance.

Predicability: In a scaling application, state management needs to stay predictable. When you alter your state, it should be clear which components care about it. It should also be clear who alters the state in the first place. In an unidirectional data flow one stakeholder alters the state, the state gets stored, and the state flows down from one place, for instance a stateful component, to all child components that are interested in the state.

Maintainability: When collaborating in a team on a scaling application, one requirement of state management is predictability. Humans are not capable to keep track of a growing bidirectional data flow. It is a limitation by nature. That's why the state management stays more maintainable when it is predictable. Otherwise, when people cannot reason about the state, they introduce inefficient state handling. But maintainability doesn't come without any cost in a unidirectional data flow. Even though the state is predictable, it often needs to be refactored thoughtfully. In a later chapter, you will read about those refactorings such as lifting state or higher-order components for local state.

Performance: In a unidirectional data flow, the state flows down the component tree. All components that depend on the state have the chance to re-render. Contrary to a bidirectional data flow, it is not always clear who has to update according to state changes. The state flows in too many directions. The model layer depends on the view layer and the view layer depends on the model layer. It's a vice versa dependency that leads to performance issues in the update lifecycle.

These three advantages show the benefits of using a unidirectional data flow over an bidirectional data flow. That's why so many state management and SPA solutions thrive for the former one nowadays.

Scaling Local State in React

You should know about all the basics in React's local state management by now. However, you will notice that there are more patterns and best practices out there to apply local state in a scaling application. The following chapter gives you insights into these topics.

Lifting State

In a scaling application, you will notice that you pass a lot of state down to child components as props. These props are often passed down multiple component levels. That's how state is shared vertically in your application. Yet, the other way around, you will notice that more components need to use and thus share the same state. That's how state needs to be shared horizontally across components in your component tree. These two scaling issues, sharing state vertically and horizontally, are common in local state management. Therefore you can lift the state up and down for keeping your local state architecture maintainable. Lifting the state prevents sharing too much or too little state in your component tree. Basically, it is a refactoring that you have to do once in a while to keep your components maintainable and focused on only consuming the state that they need to consume.

In order to experience up and down lifting of local state, the following chapter will demonstrate it with two examples. The first example that demonstrates the uplifting of state is called: "Search a List"-example. The second example that demonstrates the downlifting of state is called "Archive in a List"-example.

The "Search a List"-example has three components. Two sibling components, a `Search` component and a `List` component, that are used in an overarching `SearchableList` component. First, the implementation of the `Search` component:

Code Playground

```
import React from 'react';

class Search extends React.Component {
  constructor(props) {
    super(props);

    this.state = {
      query: ''
    };

    this.onChange = this.onChange.bind(this);
  }

  onChange(event) {
    const { value } = event.target;
```

```
    this.setState({
      query: value
    });
  }

  render() {
    return (
      <div>
        {this.props.children} <input
          type="text"
          value={this.state.query}
          onChange={this.onChange}
        />
      </div>
    );
  }
}
```

Second, the implementation of List component:

Code Playground

```
function List({ list }) {
  return (
    <ul>
      {list.map(item => <li key={item.id}>{item.name}</li>)}
    </ul>
  );
}
```

Third, the SearchableList component which uses both components, the Search and List components, and thus both components become siblings in the component tree:

Code Playground

```
function SearchableList({ list }) {
  return (
    <div>
      <Search>Search List:</Search>
      <List list={list} />
    </div>
  );
}
```

While the Search component is a stateful ES6 class component, the List component is only a stateless functional component. The parent component that combines the List and Search components into a SearchableList component is a stateless functional component too.

However, the example doesn't work. The Search component knows about the query that could be used to filter the list, but the List component doesn't know about it. The state from the Search component can only flow down the component tree by using props but not up. Therefore, you have to lift the state of the Search component up to the SearchableList to make the query state accessible for the List component in order to filter the list eventually. You want to share the query state in both List component and Search component. Whereas the Search component is responsible for altering the state, the List component consumes the state to filter the list of items. The state should be managed in the SearchableList component to make it readable and writeable for both sibling components below.

In order to lift the state up, the SearchableList becomes a stateful component. You have to refactor it to a React ES6 class component. On the other hand, you can refactor the Search component to a functional stateless component, because it doesn't need to be stateful anymore. The stateful parent component takes care about its whole state. In other cases, the Search component might stay as a stateful ES6 class component, because it still manages some other state, but it is not the case in this example. So first, that's the adjusted Search component:

Code Playground

```
function Search({ query, onChange, children }) {
  return (
    <div>
      {children} <input
        type="text"
        value={query}
        onChange={onChange}
      />
    </div>
  );
}
```

Second, the adjusted SearchableList component:

Code Playground

```
import React from 'react';

class SearchableList extends React.Component {
  constructor(props) {
    super(props);

    this.state = {
      query: ''
    };

    this.onChange = this.onChange.bind(this);
  }

  onChange(event) {
    const { value } = event.target;

    this.setState({
      query: value
    });
  }

  render() {
    const { list } = this.props;
    const { query } = this.state;

    return (
      <div>
        <Search
          query={query}
          onChange={this.onChange}
        >
          Search List:
        </Search>
        <List list={(list || []).filter(byQuery(query))} />
      </div>
    );
  }
}

function byQuery(query) {
```

```
  return function(item) {
    return !query ||
      item.name.toLowerCase().includes(query.toLowerCase());
  }
}
```

After you have lifted the state up, the parent component takes care about the local state management. Both child components don't need to take care about it. You have lifted the state up to share the local state across the child components. The list gets filtered by the search query before it reaches the List component. An alternative would be passing the query state as prop to the List component and the List component would apply the filter to the list.

In the next part, let's get to the second example: the "Archive in a List"-example. It builds up on the previous example, but this time the List component has the extended functionality to archive an item in the list. Therefore, it needs to have a button to archive an item in the list identified by an unique id property of the item. First, the enhanced List component:

Code Playground

```
function List({ list, onArchive }) {
  return (
    <ul>
      {list.map(item =>
        <li key={item.id}>
          <span>
            {item.name}
          </span>
          <span>
            <button
              type="button"
              onClick={() => onArchive(item.id)}
            >
              Archive
            </button>
          </span>
        </li>
      )}
    </ul>
  );
}
```

Second, the SearchableList component which holds the state of archived items:

Code Playground

```
import React from 'react';

class SearchableList extends React.Component {
  constructor(props) {
    super(props);

    this.state = {
      query: '',
      archivedItems: []
    };

    this.onChange = this.onChange.bind(this);
    this.onArchive = this.onArchive.bind(this);
  }

  ...

  onArchive(id) {
    const { archivedItems } = this.state;

    this.setState({
      archivedItems: [...archivedItems, id]
    });
  }

  render() {
    const { list } = this.props;
    const { query, archivedItems } = this.state;

    const filteredList = list
      .filter(byQuery(query))
      .filter(byArchived(archivedItems));

    return (
      <div>
        ...
        <List
          list={filteredList}
          onArchive={this.onArchive}
        />
      </div>
```

```
    );
  }
}

...


function byArchived(archivedItems) {
  return function(item) {
    return !archivedItems.includes(item.id);
  }
}
```

The Search component stays untouched. As you have seen, the previous example was extended to facilitate the archiving of items in a list. Now, the List component receives all the necessary properties: an onArchive() callback function and the list, filtered by query and archivedItems. It only shows items filtered by the query from the Search component and items which are not archived.

You might see already the flaw. The SearchableList takes care about the archiving functionality. However, it doesn't need the functionality itself. It only passes all the state to the List component as props. It manages the state on behalf of the List component. No other component cares about this state. In a scaling application, it would make sense to lift the state down to the List component, because only the List component cares about it and no other component has to manage it on the List component's behalf. Even though the List component becomes a stateful component afterward, it is step in the right direction keeping the local state maintainable in the long run. First, the enhanced stateful List component which takes care about the state:

Code Playground

```
import React from 'react';

class List extends React.Component {
  constructor(props) {
    super(props);

    this.state = {
      archivedItems: []
    };

    this.onArchive = this.onArchive.bind(this);
  }

  onArchive(id) {
    const { archivedItems } = this.state;
```

```
    this.setState({
      archivedItems: [...archivedItems, id]
    });
  }

  render() {
    const { list } = this.props;
    const { archivedItems } = this.state;

    const filteredList = list
      .filter(byArchived(archivedItems));

    return (
      <ul>
        {filteredList.map(item =>
          <li key={item.id}>
            <span>
              {item.name}
            </span>
            <span>
              <button
                type="button"
                onClick={() => this.onArchive(item.id)}
              >
                Archive
              </button>
            </span>
          </li>
        )}
      </ul>
    );
  }
}
```

Second, the SearchableList component which only cares about the state from the previous example but not about the archived items anymore:

Code Playground

```
import React from 'react';

class SearchableList extends React.Component {
  constructor(props) {
    super(props);

    this.state = {
      query: ''
    };

    this.onChange = this.onChange.bind(this);
  }

  ...

  render() {
    const { list } = this.props;
    const { query } = this.state;

    const filteredList = list
      .filter(byQuery(query));

    return (
      <div>
        ...
        <List list={filteredList} />
      </div>
    );
  }
}
```

That's how you can lift state down. It is used to keep the state only next to component that care about the state. Let's recap both approaches. In the first example, the "Search a List"-example, the state had to be lifted up to share the query property in two child components. The Search component had to manipulate the state by using a callback function, but also had to use the query to be a controlled component regarding the input field. On the other hand, the SearchableList component had to filter the list by using the query property on behalf of the List component. Another solution would have been to pass down the query property to the List component and let the component deal with the filtering itself. After all, the state got lifted up the component tree to share it vertically across more components.

In the second example, the "Archive in a List"-example, the state could be lifted down to keep the state maintainable in the long run. The parent component shouldn't be concerned about state that isn't used by the parent component itself and isn't shared across multiple child components. Because only one child component cared about the archived items, it was a good change to lift the state down to the only component which cares about the state. After all, the state got lifted down the component tree.

In conclusion, lifting state allows you to keep your local state management maintainable. **Lifting state should be used to give components access to all the state they need, but not to more state than they need.** Sometimes you have to refactor components from a functional stateless component to a React ES6 class component or vice versa. It's not always possible, because a component that could become possibly a stateless functional component could still have other stateful properties.

Functional State

In the recent chapters you have used `this.setState()` to alter the local state. However, there is a flaw in using `this.setState()` the way we did in the last chapters for certain use cases: It is important to know that `this.setState()` is executed asynchronously to update the local state. React batches all the state updates, because it executes them after each other for performance optimizations. Thus, the `this.setState()` method comes in two versions.

In its first version, the `this.setState()` method takes an object to update the state. As explained in a previous chapter, the merging of the object is a shallow merge. For instance, when updating `authors` in a state object of `authors` and `articles`, the `articles` stay intact. The previous examples have already used this approach:

Code Playground

```
this.setState({
  ...
});
```

In its second version, the `this.setState()` method takes a function as argument. The function has the previous state and props in the function signature to be used for the state update.

Code Playground

```
this.setState((prevState, props) => ({
  ...
}));
```

So, what's the flaw in using `this.setState()` with an object? In several examples in the last chapters, the state was updated based on the previous state or props. However, `this.setState()`

executes asynchronously. Thus the state or props that are used to perform the update could be stale at this point in time, because the state was updated more than once in between. It could lead to bugs in your local state management, because you would update the state based on stale properties. When using the functional approach to update the local state, the state and props are used when `this.setState()` performs asynchronously at the time of its execution. Let's revisit one of the previous examples:

Code Playground

```
import React from 'react';

class CounterContainer extends React.Component {
  constructor(props) {
    super(props);

    this.state = {
      counter: 0
    };

    this.onIncrement = this.onIncrement.bind(this);
    this.onDecrement = this.onDecrement.bind(this);
  }

  onIncrement() {
    this.setState({
      counter: this.state.counter + 1
    });
  }

  onDecrement() {
    this.setState({
      counter: this.state.counter - 1
    });
  }

  render() {
    return <CounterPresenter
      counter={this.state.counter}
      onIncrement={this.onIncrement}
      onDecrement={this.onDecrement}
    />
  }
}
```

Executing one of the class methods, onIncrement() or onDecrement(), multiple times could lead to a bug. Because both methods depend on the previous state, it could use a stale state when the asynchronous update wasn't executed in between and the method got invoked another time.

Code Playground

```
this.setState({ counter: this.state.counter + 1 }); // this.state: { counter: 0 }
this.setState({ counter: this.state.counter + 1 }); // this.state: { counter: 0 }
this.setState({ counter: this.state.counter + 1 }); // this.state: { counter: 0 }
// updated state: { counter: 1 }
// instead of: { counter: 3 }
```

It becomes even more error prone when multiple functions, such as onIncrement() and onDecrement(), that use this.setState() depend on the previous state. You can refactor the example to use the functional state updating approach:

Code Playground

```
import React from 'react';

class CounterContainer extends React.Component {
  constructor(props) {
    ...
  }

  onIncrement() {
    this.setState(prevState => ({
      counter: prevState.counter + 1
    }));
  }

  onDecrement() {
    this.setState(prevState => ({
      counter: prevState.counter - 1
    }));
  }

  render() {
    ...
  }
}
```

The functional approach opens up two more benefits. First, the function which is used in this.setState() is a pure function. There are no side-effects. The function always will return the same output (next state) when given the same input (previous state). It makes it predictable and uses the benefits of functional programming. Second, since the function is pure, it can be tested easily in an unit test and independently from the component. It gives you the opportunity to test your local state updates as business logic which is separated from the view layer. You only have to extract the function from the component.

Code Playground

```
import React from 'react';

const incrementUpdate = prevState => ({
  counter: prevState.counter + 1
});

const decrementUpdate = prevState => ({
  counter: prevState.counter - 1
});

class CounterContainer extends React.Component {
  constructor(props) {
    ...
  }

  onIncrement() {
    this.setState(incrementUpdate);
  }

  onDecrement() {
    this.setState(decrementUpdate);
  }

  render() {
    ...
  }
}
```

Now, you could test the pure functions as business logic separately from the view layer. After all you may wonder when to use the object and when to use the function in this.setState()? The recommended rules of thumb are:

- Always use this.setState() with a function when you depend on previous state or props.
- Only use this.setState() with an object when you don't depend on previous properties.
- In case of uncertainty, default to use this.setState() with a function.

Higher-Order Components

Higher-order components (HOCs) can be used for a handful of use cases. One of these use case would be to enable an elegant way of conditional rendering[34]. But this book is about state management, so why not use it to manage the local state of a component? Let's revisit an adjusted example of the "Archive in a List"-example.

Code Playground

```
import React from 'react';

class ArchiveableList extends React.Component {
  constructor(props) {
    super(props);

    this.state = {
      archivedItems: []
    };

    this.onArchive = this.onArchive.bind(this);
  }

  onArchive(id) {
    const { archivedItems } = this.state;

    this.setState({
      archivedItems: [...archivedItems, id]
    });
  }

  render() {
    const { list } = this.props;
    const { archivedItems } = this.state;

    const filteredList = list
      .filter(byArchived(archivedItems));

    return (
      <ul>
        {filteredList.map(item =>
          <li key={item.id}>
            <span>
```

---

[34]https://www.robinwieruch.de/gentle-introduction-higher-order-components/

```
          {item.name}
        </span>
        <span>
          <button
            type="button"
            onClick={() => onArchive(item.id)}
          >
            Archive
          </button>
        </span>
      </li>
    )}
  </ul>
  );
  }
}


function byArchived(archivedItems) {
  return function(item) {
    return !archivedItems.includes(item.id);
  };
}
```

The `ArchiveableList` component has two purposes. On the one hand, it is a pure presenter component that shows the items in a list. On the other hand, it is stateful container component that keeps track of the archived items. Therefore, you could split this two responsibilities up into representation and logic thus into presentational and container component. It would be the same refactoring you have done before with the `CounterContainer` and `CounterPresenter` components. However, another approach could be to transfer the logic, in this case the local state management, into a higher-order component. Higher-order components are reusable and thus the local state management could become reusable for many components but not only one.

Code Playground

```
import React from 'react';

function byArchived(archivedItems) {
  return function(item) {
    return !archivedItems.includes(item.id);
  };
}


function withArchive(Component) {
```

```
class WithArchive extends React.Component {
  constructor(props) {
    super(props);

    this.state = {
      archivedItems: []
    };

    this.onArchive = this.onArchive.bind(this);
  }

  onArchive(id) {
    const { archivedItems } = this.state;

    this.setState({
      archivedItems: [...archivedItems, id]
    });
  }

  render() {
    const { list } = this.props;
    const { archivedItems } = this.state;

    const filteredList = list
      .filter(byArchived(archivedItems));

    return <Component
      list={filteredList}
      onArchive={this.onArchive}
    />
  }
}

return WithArchive;
}
```

In return the List component would only display the list and receives a function in its props to archive an item.

Code Playground

```
function List({ list, onArchive }) {
  return (
    <ul>
      {list.map(item =>
        <li key={item.id}>
          <span>
            {item.name}
          </span>
          <span>
            <button
              type="button"
              onClick={() => onArchive(item.id)}
            >
              Archive
            </button>
          </span>
        </li>
      )}
    </ul>
  );
}
```

Now you can compose the list facilitating component with the functionality to archive items in a list.

Code Playground

```
import React from 'react';

function byArchived(archivedItems) { ... }

function withArchive(Component) { ... }

function List({ list, onArchive }) { ... }

const ListWithArchive = withArchive(List);

function App({ list }) {
  return <ListWithArchive list={list} />
}
```

The `List` component would only display the items. The ability to archive an item in the `List` component would be opt-in with a higher-order component called `withArchive`. In addition, the HOC can be reused in other `List` components too for managing the state of archived items. After all, higher-order components are great to extract local state management from components and to reuse the local state management logic in other components.

React's Context for Provider and Consumer

The context API is a powerful feature in React. You will not often see it when using plain React, but might consider using it when your React application grows in size and depth from a component perspective. Basically, React's context API takes the clutter away of passing mandatory props, that are needed by every component, down your whole component tree. Most often components in between are not interested in these props.

But you will not only see it when using plain React. Often React's context API can be seen in action when using an external state management library such as Redux or MobX. There, you often end up with a `Provider` component at the top of your component hierarchy that bridges your state layer (Redux/MobX/...) to your view layer (React). The `Provider` component receives the state as props and afterward, each child component has implicitly access to the managed state by Redux and MobX.

Do you remember the last time when you had to pass props several components down your component tree? In plain React, you can be confronted often with this issue which is called "prop drilling". It can happen that a couple of these props are even mandatory for each child component. Thus you would need to pass the props down to each child component. In return, this would clutter every component in between which has to pass down these props without using them oneself.

When these props become mandatory, React's context API gives you a way out of this mess. Instead of passing down the props explicitly down to each component, you can hide props, that are necessary for each component, in React's context and pass them implicitly down to each component. React's context traverses invisible down the component tree. If a component needs access to the context, it can consume it on demand.

What are use cases for this approach? For instance, your application could have a configurable colored theme. Each component should be colored depending on the configuration. The configuration is fetched once from your server, but afterward you want to make this implicitly accessible for all components. Therefore you could use React's context API to give every component access to the colored theme. You would have to provide the colored theme at the top of your component hierarchy and consume it in every component which is located somewhere below it.

How is React's context provided and consumed? Imagine you would have component A as root component that provides the context and component C as one of the child components that consumes the context. Somewhere in between is component D though. The application has a colored theme that can be used to style your components. Your goal is it to make the colored theme available for every component via the React context. In this case, component C should be able to consume it.

First, you have to create the context which gives you access to a Provider and Consumer component. When you create the context with React by using `createContext()`, you can pass it an initial value. In this case, the initial value can be null, because you may have no access to the initial value at this point in time. Otherwise, you can already give it here a proper initial value.

Code Playground

```
import React from 'react';

const ThemeContext = React.createContext(null);

export default ThemeContext;
```

Second, the A component would have to provide the context. It is a hardcoded `value` in this case, but it can be anything from component state or component props. The context value may change as well when the local state is changed due to a `setState()` call. Component A displays only component D yet makes the context available to all its other components below it. One of the leaf components will be component C that consumes the context eventually.

Code Playground

```
import ThemeContext from './ThemeContext';

class A extends React.Component {
  render() {
    return (
      <ThemeContext.Provider value={'green'}>
        <D />
      </ThemeContext.Provider>
    );
  }
}
```

Third, in your component C, somewhere below component D, you can consume the context object. Notice that component A doesn't need to pass down anything via component D in the props so that it reaches component C.

Code Playground

```
import ThemeContext from './ThemeContext';

class C extends React.Component {
  render() {
    return (
      <ThemeContext.Consumer>
        {coloredTheme =>
          <div style={{ color: coloredTheme }}>
            Hello World
          </div>
        }
      </ThemeContext.Consumer>
    );
  }
}
```

The component can derive its style by consuming the context. The Consumer component makes the passed context available by using a {{% a_blank "render prop" "https://reactjs.org/docs/render-props.html" %}}. As you can imagine, following this way every component that needs to be styled accordingly to the colored theme could get the necessary information from React's context API by using the Consumer component now. You only have to use the Provider component which passes the value once somewhere above them and then consume it with the Consumer component. You can read more about React's context API in the official documentation[35].

That's basically it for React's context API. You have one Provider component that makes properties accessible in React's context and components that consume the context by using the Consumer component. How does this relate to state management? Basically the pattern, also called provider pattern, is often applied, when using a sophisticated state management solution that makes the state object(s) accessible in your view layer via React's context. Thus the whole state can be accessed in each component. Perhaps you will never implement the provider pattern yourself, but you will most likely use it in a sophisticated state management solution such as Redux or MobX later on. So keep it in mind. Otherwise, React's context can be used to store a state object itself. It can be used when the state is shared globally in your React application, but you don't want to introduce Redux or MobX yet.

---

[35]https://reactjs.org/docs/context.html

Persistence in State

State in applications is often not persistent. When your application starts, there is often an initial state, but there is not database to recreate the state from a previous session. However, in your application the state updates when the user interacts with the application (local data) or data arrives from a backend application (remote data). You may wonder whether there is a way to persist the state so that it can be used as initial state when the application starts again. The question applies to both, local state management and sophisticated state management later on.

The obvious answer to this question would be to implement a backend application with a database to persist the state. Extracting the state from your application is called **dehydrating state**. Now, every time your application starts again, you would retrieve the state from the backend application. Once the state arrives in the response asynchronously, you would **rehydrate state** into your application again. That's how you would achieve the initial application state from a persisted database.

While the dehydration of the state could happen any time your application is running, perhaps when the user interacts with your application, the rehydration would take place when your components mount when starting your application. The best place to do it in React would be the component-DidMount() lifecycle method. Take for example the ArchiveableList component from a previous chapter. It could retrieve all the archived unique identifiers of items on componentDidMount() from your backend application and rehydrate them to the local state.

Code Playground

```
import React from 'react';

class ArchiveableList extends React.Component {
  constructor(props) {
    ...
  }

  onArchive(id) {
    ...
  }

  componentDidMount() {
    fetch('path/to/archived/items')
      .then(response => response.json())
      .then(archivedItems => this.setState(rehydrateArchivedItems(archivedItems)\
));
  }

  render() {
    ...
```

```
  }
}

function rehydrateArchivedItems(archivedItems) {
  return function(prevState) {
    return {
      archivedItems: [
        ...prevState.archivedItems,
        ...archivedItems
      ]
    };
  };
}
```

Now, every time the component initializes, the persistent archived items will be used as initial state for your component. In fact, the initial state is defined in the constructor of the component, but after the component mounted it fetches the next state from the backend application and rehydrates it as initial state.

On the other side, the dehydration could happen anytime, but to avoid inconsistencies, in the example of archived items, the dehydration would take place when an item gets archived. It is a usual request to the backend to save the item as being archived.

The rehydration and dehydration of state are most often unconscious steps in modern applications. It is common sense to retrieve all the necessary data from the backend when your application starts and to update the data when something has changed. But you can keep the rehydration and dehydration of state in mind to keep your application state in sync with your backend data as single source of truth.

Local Storage

You may wonder whether there is a more lightweight solution compared to a backend application? Yes there is one: You could use the native browser API. To be more specific, most of the modern browsers have a storage functionality to persist data. It is the lightweight version of a database that is used in the browser. Of course, it is only visible to the user of the browser and cannot be distributed to other users. And once users clear their browser data, the store is cleared as well. So in real the data is not fully persistent, but at least can be used between browser sessions.

Modern browsers have access to the local storage[36] and session storage[37]. Both work the same, but there is one difference in their functionalities. While the local storage keeps the data even when the browser is closed, the session storage expires once the browser closes. Both storages work the same by using key value pairs.

---

[36]https://developer.mozilla.org/en/docs/Web/API/Window/localStorage
[37]https://developer.mozilla.org/en/docs/Web/API/Window/sessionStorage

Code Playground

```
// Save data to localStorage
localStorage.setItem('key', 'value');

// Get saved data from localStorage
var data = localStorage.getItem('key');

// Remove saved data from localStorage
localStorage.removeItem('key');

// Remove all saved data from localStorage
localStorage.clear();
```

In the end, you can apply them the same way as you did in the previous `ArchiveableList` component that used the request to a backend application to retrieve the data. Now the `ArchiveableList` component would use the storage instead of the backend to retrieve the state. If you are keen to explore the usage with the local storage in React, you can read more about it in this article: How to use Local Storage in React[38].

Caching in State

The local state, later on the sophisticated state as well, can be used as a cache for your application. A cache would make recurring requests to retrieve data from a backend redundant, because they would return the same data as before and the data is already cached in the state.

Imagine your application has an interface to search for popular stories on a news platform. The news platform has an open API that you can use to retrieve those popular stories. Your own application that consumes the API of this platform would only have a search field to search for popular stories from the platform and a list to display the stories once you have searched for them.

Next, imagine you made your first request searching popular stories about "React". You are not satisfied with the search result, because you wanted to be more specific, and search again for "React Local State". Still, no satisfying search result, but the search result for "React Local State" is visible in your application. Next, you want to head back to search for "React" stories again. Your application makes a third request to retrieve the "React" stories from the third-party API. In a perfect world, the application would know that you have already searched for "React" stories before. That's where caching comes into play. The third request could have been avoided if the application had cached the search results.

Such a fluctuant cache solution is not too difficult to implement with a local state. Bear in mind that it would work with a sophisticated state management solution, such as Redux or MobX, too. So

---

[38]https://www.robinwieruch.de/local-storage-react/

when searching for the stories, you already have a unique identifier which you can use as a key in an object to store the search result in the local state. The unique identifier is your search term. It would be either "React" or "React Local State" considering the previous example. The value corresponding to the key would be the search result. In the example, it would be the popular stories about "React" and "React Local Storage". After all, your cache object in the local state might be similar to this:

Code Playground

```
this.state = {
  ...
  searchCache: {
    React: [...],
    ReactLocalState: [...],
  }
}
```

Every time your application performs a search request, the key value pair in the cache object in your local state would be filled. Before you make a new request, the cache would be checked whether the search term is already available as a key in the object. If the key is available, the request would be suppressed and the cache result would be used instead. If the key is not available, a request would be made. After the request succeeded, the search term would be saved as key and the search result would be saved as value for the key in the local state.

The book doesn't give you an in-depth implementation of the cache solution. If you did read the Road to learn React[39], you will already know how to implement such a cache in plain React with local state. In one of its lessons, the book uses a cache in a more elaborated way to cache even paginated search results efficiently in the local state. So if you are interested in it, checkout "the Road to learn React"-book again.

---

[39]https://www.robinwieruch.de/the-road-to-learn-react/

Transition to Sophisticated State

By now you have learned about the basics in local state management and how to scale it in a growing application with a variety of techniques and best practices. These learnings should give you a great surface area to apply them in your applications to scale state management without using a sophisticated state management library and by only using local state. So what's next in this book? The following chapters will give you a transition from local state management to sophisticated state management.

The Controversies of Local State Management

State management is a controversial topic. You will find a ton of discussions and opinions around it. You will find it as recurring topic not only in React, but also in other SPA or view layer solutions for modern web applications. The book is my attempt to give you consistency for these opinions and enable you to learn state management step by step.

The following statement is controversial: *The local state in React is sufficient for most of your application. You will not need a sophisticated state management solutions like Redux or MobX.*

Personally, I agree with the statement. You can build quite large applications with only local state management. You should be aware of best practices and patterns to scale it, as you have learned them in the previous chapters, but it is doable. You can spare a lot of application complexity by using plain local state. Once your application scales, you might want to consider using a sophisticated state management library at some point.

The next statement might be controversial, too: *Once you have a sophisticated state management library in place, you shouldn't use local state anymore.*

Personally, I strongly disagree with the statement. Not every state should live in a sophisticated state management. There are many use cases when local state is applicable in large applications. Especially when considering entity state and view state: The view state can most often live in a local state, because it is not shared widely across the application. But the entity state most likely lives in a sophisticated state, because it is shared across multiple components. It might need to be accessible and modifiable by multiple components across your application.

Last but not least, another controversial statement: *You don't need React's local state, you can learn Redux instead altogether with React.*

I strongly disagree with the statement, too. If you want to develop applications with React, you should certainly be aware of local state in React. You should have built applications with it before you start to learn and apply sophisticated state management solutions. You need to run into local state management problems before you get the help of sophisticated state management solutions. You will always need local state management, even for large applications.

These were only three controversial statements. But there are way more opinions around the topic. In the end, you should make your own experiences to get to know what makes sense to you. However, if you are transitioning from plain React to React + Redux or React + Redux, I highly recommend reading this article before continuing reading the book: Things to learn in React before using Redux[40].

The Flaw of Local State Management

In order to come to a conclusion of local state management, there is one open question: What's the problem with local state management? Developers wonder why they need sophisticated state management in order to tame their state. In other scenarios, people never wonder about it, because they have learned sophisticated state management from the beginning without using local state. That might not be the best approach in the first place, because you have to experience a problem before you use a solution for it. You can't skip the problem and use the solution right away.

So what's the problem with using only local state management? It doesn't scale in large applications. It doesn't scale implementation-wise, but it probably doesn't scale in a team of developers too.

Implementation-wise it doesn't scale because too many components across your application share state. They need to access the state, need to modify it or need to remove it. In a small application, these components are not far away from each other. You can apply best practices like lifting state up and down to keep the state management maintainable. At some point, components are too far away from each other. The state needs to be lifted the component tree all the way up. Still, child components could be multiple levels below the stateful component. The state would creep through all components in between even though these components don't need access to it. That's there you may want to consider React's context API, but it shouldn't replace your whole state management architecture.

Local state can become unmaintainable. It is already difficult for one person to keep the places in mind where local state is used in the component tree. When a team of developers implements one application, it becomes even more difficult to keep track of it. Usually it is not necessary to keep track about the local state. In a perfect world, everyone would lift state up and down to keep it maintainable. In the real world, code doesn't get refactored as often as it should be. The state creeps through all components even though they don't consume it.

One could argue that the issues of maintainability apply for sophisticated state as well. That's true, there are pitfalls again that people need to avoid to keep the state management maintainable. For instance, not every component should know about the global state. However, at least the state management is gathered at one place, in a global state, to maintain it. It doesn't get too mixed up with the view layer. There are only bridges that connect the view layer with the state layer. Thus it is a wise decision to apply sophisticated state management in larger applications in order to tame the state. So let's get into it!

---

[40]https://www.robinwieruch.de/learn-react-before-using-redux/

Redux

Redux is one of the libraries that helps you implement sophisticated state management in your applications. It goes beyond the local state (e.g. React's local state). It is one of the solutions you would take in a scaling application in order to tame the state. A React application is a perfect fit for Redux, yet other libraries and frameworks highly adopted its concepts as well.

Why is Redux that popular in the JavaScript community? In order to answer that question, I have to go a bit into the past of JavaScript applications. In the beginning, there was one library to rule them all: jQuery. It was mainly used to manipulate the DOM, to amaze with animations and to implement reusable widgets. It was the number one library in JavaScript. There was no way around it. However, the usage of jQuery skyrocketed and applications grew in size. But not in size of HTML and CSS, it was rather the size of code in JavaScript. Eventually, the code in those applications became a mess, because there was no proper architecture or frame around it. The infamous spaghetti code became a problem in JavaScript applications.

It was about time for nouveau solutions to emerge which would go beyond jQuery. These libraries, most of them frameworks, would bring the tools for proper architectures in frontend applications. In addition, they would bring opinionated approaches to solve problems. These solutions enabled developers to implement single page applications (SPAs).

Single page applications became popular when the first generation of frameworks and libraries, among them Angular 1, Ember and Backbone, were released. Suddenly, developers had frameworks to build scaling frontend applications. However, as history repeats itself, with every new technology there will be new problems. In SPAs every solution had a different approach for state management. For instance, Angular 1 used the infamous two-way data binding. It embraced a bidirectional data flow. Only after applications grew in size, the problem of state management became widely known.

During that time React was released by Facebook. It was among the second generation of SPA solutions. Compared to the first generation, it was a library that only leveraged the view layer. It came with an own state management solution though: React's local state management.

In React, the principle of the unidirectional data flow became popular. State management should be more predictable in order to reason about it. Yet, the local state management wasn't sufficient at some point. React applications scaled very well, but ran into the same problems of predictable and maintainable state management when building larger applications. Even though the problems weren't as destructive as in bidirectional data flow applications, there was still a problem once the application got larger. That was the time when Facebook introduced the Flux architecture.

The Flux architecture is a pattern to deal with state management in scaling applications. The official website says that *"[a] unidirectional data flow is central to the Flux pattern [...]"*. The data flows only in one direction. Apart from the unidirectional data flow, the Flux architecture came with four essential components: Action, Dispatcher, Store and View. The View is basically the component tree in a modern application. For instance, React is such a View. A user can interact with the View in order to trigger an Action. An Action would encapsulate all the necessary information to update the state in the Store(s). The Dispatcher on the way delegates the Actions to the Store(s). The new state would be propagated from the Store(s) to the View to update them. The last part closes the loop of the unidirectional data flow.

The data flow goes in one direction. A View can trigger an Action, that goes through the Dispatcher and Store, and would change the View eventually when the state in the Store changed. The unidirectional data flow is enclosed in this loop. Then again, a View can trigger another Action. Since Facebook introduced the Flux architecture, the View was associated with React and its components.

You can read more about the Flux architecture on the official website[41]. There you will find a video about its introduction at a conference[42] too. If you are interested about the origins of Redux, I highly recommend reading and watching the material. After all, Redux became the successor library of the Flux architecture. Even though there were a bunch of solutions around the Flux architecture, Redux managed to surpass them. But why did it succeed?

Dan Abramov[43] and Andrew Clark[44] are the creators of Redux. It was introduced by Dan Abramov at React Europe[45] in 2015. However, the talk by Dan doesn't introduce Redux per se. Instead, the talk introduced a problem that Dan Abramov faced that led to implementing Redux. I don't want to foreclose the content of the talk, that's why I encourage you to watch the video yourself. If you are keen to learn Redux, you should dive into the problem that was solved by it.

Nevertheless, one year later, again at React Europe, Dan Abramov reflected on the journey of Redux and its success. He mentioned a few things that had made Redux successful in his opinion. First, Redux was developed to solve a problem. The problem was explained by Dan Abramov one year earlier when he introduced Redux. It was not yet another library. It was a library that solved a problem. Time Traveling and Hot Reloading were the stress test for Redux. Second, the constraints of Redux were another key factor to its success. Redux managed to shield away the problem with a simple API and a thoughtful way to solve the problem of state management itself. You can watch this talk[46] too. I highly recommend it. Either you watch it right now or after the next chapter that introduces you to the basics of Redux.

---

[41]https://facebook.github.io/flux/

[42]https://youtu.be/nYkdrAPrdcw?list=PLb0IAmt7-GS188xDYE-u1ShQmFFGbrk0v

[43]https://twitter.com/dan_abramov

[44]https://twitter.com/acdlite

[45]https://www.youtube.com/watch?v=xsSnOQynTHs

[46]https://www.youtube.com/watch?v=uvAXVMwHJXU

Basics in Redux

On the official Redux website[47] it says: *"Redux is a predictable state container for JavaScript apps."*. It can be used standalone or in connection with with libraries, like React and Angular, to manage state in JavaScript applications.

Redux adopted a handful of constraints from the Flux architecture but not all of them. It has Actions that encapsulate information for the actual state update. It has a Store to save the state, too. However, the Store is a singleton. Thus, there are not multiple Stores like there used to be in the Flux architecture. In addition, there is no single Dispatcher. Instead, Redux uses multiple Reducers. Basically, Reducers pick up the information from Actions and "reduce" the information to a new state, along with the old state, that is stored in the Store. When state in the Store is changed, the View can act on this by subscribing to the Store.

Concept Playground

```
View -> Action -> Reducer(s) -> Store -> View
```

So why is it called Redux? Because it combines the two words Reducer and Flux. The abstract picture of Redux should be imaginable now. The state doesn't live in the View anymore, it is only connected to the View. What does connected mean? It is connected on two ends, because it is part of the unidirectional data flow. One end is responsible to trigger an Action to which updates the state eventually and the second end is responsible to receive the state from the Store. Therefore, the View can update according to state changes and can trigger state changes. The View, in this case, would be React, but Redux can be used with any other library or standalone as well. After all, it is only a state management container.

Action(s)

An action in Redux is a JavaScript object. It has a type and an optional payload. The type is often referred to as **action type**. While the type is a string literal, the payload can be anything from a string to an object.

In the beginning your playground to get to know Redux will be a Todo application. For instance, the following action in this application can be used to add a new todo item:

---

[47]http://redux.js.org

Code Playground

```
{
  type: 'TODO_ADD',
  todo: { id: '0', name: 'learn redux', completed: false },
}
```

Executing an action is called **dispatching** in Redux. You can dispatch an action to alter the state in the Redux store. You only dispatch an action when you want to change the state. The dispatching of an action can be triggered in your view layer. It could be as simple as a click on a HTML button. In addition, the payload in a Redux action is not mandatory. You can define actions that have only an action type. That subject will be revisited later in the book. In the end, once an action is dispatched, it will go through all reducers in Redux.

Reducer(s)

A reducer is the next part in the chain of the unidirectional data flow. The view dispatches an action and the action object, with action type and optional payload, will pass through all reducers. What's a reducer? A reducer is a pure function. It always produces the same output when the input stays the same. It has no side-effects, thus it is only an input/output operation. A reducer has two inputs: state and action. The state is always the whole state object from the Redux store. The action is the dispatched action with a type and an optional payload. The reducer reduces - that explains the naming - the previous state and incoming action to a new state.

Code Playground

```
(prevState, action) => newState
```

Apart from the functional programming principle, namely that a reducer is a pure function without side-effects, it also embraces immutable data structures. It always returns a newState object without mutating the incoming prevState object. Thus, the following reducer, where the state of the Todo application is a list of todos, is not an allowed reducer function:

Code Playground

```
function(state, action) {
  state.push(action.todo);
  return state;
}
```

It would mutate the previous state instead of returning a new state object. The following is allowed because it keeps the previous state intact:

Code Playground

```
function reducer(state, action) {
  return state.concat(action.todo);
}
```

By using the JavaScript built-in concat functionality[48], the state and thus the list of todos is concatenated to another item. The other item is the newly added todo from the action. You might wonder if this embraces immutability now. Yes it does, because concat always returns a new array without mutating the old array. The data structure stays immutable. You will learn more about how to keep your data structures immutable later in this book.

But what about the action type? Right now, only the payload is used to produce a new state but the action type is ignored. So what can you do about the action type? Basically when an action object arrives at the reducers, the action type can be evaluated. Only when a reducer cares about the action type, it will produce a new state. Otherwise, it simply returns the previous state. In JavaScript, a switch case can help to evaluate different action types. Otherwise, it returns the previous state as default.

Imagine your Todo application would have a second action that toggles a Todo to either completed or incomplete. The only information which is needed as payload is an identifier to identify the Todo in the state.

Code Playground

```
{
  type: 'TODO_TOGGLE',
  todo: { id: '0' },
}
```

The reducer would have to act on two actions now: TODO_ADD and TODO_TOGGLE. By using a switch case statement, you can branch into different cases. If there is not such a case, you return the unchanged state by default.

---

[48]https://developer.mozilla.org/en/docs/Web/JavaScript/Reference/Global_Objects/Array/concat

Code Playground

```
function reducer(state, action) {
  switch(action.type) {
    case 'TODO_ADD' : {
      // do something and return new state
    }
    case 'TODO_TOGGLE' : {
      // do something and return new state
    }
    default : return state;
  }
}
```

The book already discussed the TODO_ADD action type and its functionality. It simply concats a new todo item to the previous list of todo items. But what about the TODO_TOGGLE functionality?

Code Playground

```
function reducer(state, action) {
  switch(action.type) {
    case 'TODO_ADD' : {
      return state.concat(action.todo);
    }
    case 'TODO_TOGGLE' : {
      return state.map(todo =>
        todo.id === action.todo.id
          ? Object.assign({}, todo, { completed: !todo.completed })
          : todo
      );
    }
    default : return state;
  }
}
```

In the example, the built-in JavaScript functionality map is used to map over the state, the list of todos, to either return the intact todo or return the toggled todo. The toggled todo is identified by its id property. The JavaScript built-in functionality map[49] always returns a new array. It doesn't mutate the previous state and thus the state of todos stays immutable and can be returned as a new state.

---

[49]https://developer.mozilla.org/en/docs/Web/JavaScript/Reference/Global_Objects/Array/map

But isn't the toggled todo mutated? No, because `Object.assign()` returns a new object without mutating the old object. `Object.assign()` merges all given objects from the former to the latter into each other. If a former object shares the same property as a latter object, the property of the latter object will be used. Thus, the `completed` property of the updated todo item will be the negated state of the old todo item.

Note that these functionalities, actions and reducer, are plain JavaScript. There is no function from the Redux library involved so far. There is no hidden library magic. It is plain JavaScript with functional programming principles in mind.

There is one useful thing to know about the current reducer: It has grown in size that makes it less maintainable. In order to keep reducers tidy, often the different switch case branches are extracted as pure functions:

Code Playground

```
function reducer(state, action) {
  switch(action.type) {
    case 'TODO_ADD' : {
      return applyAddTodo(state, action);
    }
    case 'TODO_TOGGLE' : {
      return applyToggleTodo(state, action);
    }
    default : return state;
  }
}

function applyAddTodo(state, action) {
  return state.concat(action.todo);
}

function applyToggleTodo(state, action) {
  return state.map(todo =>
    todo.id === action.todo.id
      ? Object.assign({}, todo, { completed: !todo.completed })
      : todo
  );
}
```

In the end, the Todo application has two actions and one reducer by now. One last part in the Redux setup is missing: the Store.

Store

So far, the Todo application has a way to trigger state updates (actions) and a way to reduce the previous state and action to a new state (reducer). But no one is responsible to glue these parts together.

- Who delegates the actions to the reducer?
- Who triggers actions?
- And finally: Where do I get the updated state to glue it to my View?

It is the Redux store. The store holds one global state object. There are no multiple stores and no multiple states. The store is only one instance in your application. In addition, it is the first library dependency you encounter when using Redux. Therefore, use the import statement to get the functionality to create the store object from the Redux library.

Code Playground

```
import { createStore } from 'redux';
```

Now you can use it to create a store singleton instance. The createStore function takes one mandatory argument: a reducer. You already defined a reducer in the Reducer chapter which adds and completes todo items.

Code Playground

```
const store = createStore(reducer);
```

In addition, the createStore takes a second optional argument: the initial state. In the case of the Todo application, the reducer operated on a list of todos as state. The list of todo items should be initialized as an empty array or pre-filled array with todos. If it wasn't initialized, the reducer would fail because it would operate on an undefined argument.

Code Playground

```
const store = createStore(reducer, []);
```

In another chapter, the book will showcase another way to initialize state in Redux. Then you will use the reducer instead of the store to initialize state on a more fine-grained level.

Now you have a store instance that knows about the reducer. The Redux setup is done. However, the essential part is missing: You want to interact with the store. You want to dispatch actions to alter the state, get the state from the store and listen to updates of the state in the store.

So first, how to dispatch an action?

Code Playground

```
store.dispatch({
  type: 'TODO_ADD',
  todo: { id: '0', name: 'learn redux', completed: false },
});
```

Second: How to get the global state from the store?

Code Playground

```
store.getState();
```

And third, how to subscribe (and unsubscribe) to the store in order to listen (and unlisten) for updates?

Code Playground

```
const unsubscribe = store.subscribe(() => {
  console.log(store.getState());
});

unsubscribe();
```

That's all to it. The Redux store has only a slim API to access the state, update it and listen for updates. It is one of the essential constraints which made Redux so successful.

Hands On: Redux Standalone

You know about all the basics in Redux now. A view dispatches an action on the store, the action passes all reducers and gets reduced by reducers that care about it. The store saves the new state object. Finally, a listener updates the view with the new state.

Concept Playground

```
View -> Action -> Reducer(s) -> Store -> View
```

Let's apply these learnings. You can either use your own project where you have JavaScript, JavaScript ES6 features enabled and Redux, or you can open up the following JS Bin: Redux Playground[50]. Now you are going to apply your learnings about actions, reducers, and the store from the last chapter. First, you can define your reducer that deals with adding and toggling todo items:

---

[50]https://jsbin.com/zukogaj/2/edit?html,js,console

Code Playground

```
function reducer(state, action) {
  switch(action.type) {
    case 'TODO_ADD' : {
      return applyAddTodo(state, action);
    }
    case 'TODO_TOGGLE' : {
      return applyToggleTodo(state, action);
    }
    default : return state;
  }
}

function applyAddTodo(state, action) {
  return state.concat(action.todo);
}

function applyToggleTodo(state, action) {
  return state.map(todo =>
    todo.id === action.todo.id
      ? Object.assign({}, todo, { completed: !todo.completed })
      : todo
  );
}
```

Second, you can initialize the Redux store that uses the reducer and an initial state. In the JS Bin you have Redux available as global variable.

Code Playground

```
const store = Redux.createStore(reducer, []);
```

If you are in your own project, you might be able to import the createStore from the Redux library:

Code Playground

```
import { createStore } from 'redux';

const store = createStore(reducer, []);
```

Third, you can dispatch your first action on the store.

Code Playground

```
store.dispatch({
  type: 'TODO_ADD',
  todo: { id: '0', name: 'learn redux', completed: false },
});
```

That's it. You have set up all parts of Redux and interacted with it by using an action. You can retrieve the state by getting it from the store now.

Code Playground

```
console.log(store.getState());
```

But rather than outputting it manually, you can subscribe a callback function to the store to output the latest state after it has changed. Make sure to subscribe to the store before dispatching your actions in order to get the output.

Code Playground

```
const unsubscribe = store.subscribe(() => {
  console.log(store.getState());
});
```

Now, whenever you dispatch an action, after the state got updated, the store subscription should become active by outputting your current state. Don't forget to unsubscribe eventually to avoid memory leaks.

Code Playground

```
unsubscribe();
```

A finished application can be found in this JS Bin[51]. Before you continue to read, you should experiment with the project. What you see in the project is plain JavaScript with a Redux store. You can come up with more actions and deal with them in your reducer. The application should make you aware that Redux is only a state container. The state can be altered by using actions. The reducer take care of the action. It uses the action and the old state to create a new state in the Redux store.

Later you will learn about how to to connect the Redux store to your React view layer. But before doing so, let's dive into actions and reducers a bit deeper.

---

[51]https://jsbin.com/kopohur/28/edit?html,js,console

Advanced Actions

You have learned about actions in a previous chapter. However, there are more fine-grained details that I want to cover in this chapter. The same applies for reducers. Both concepts will be covered in the following chapters in more detail. Therefore, it would be a requirement that you feel confident with the learnings from the previous chapter. Not all of the following learnings are mandatory to write applications in Redux, but they teach best practices and common usage patterns. In a larger sized application, you would want to know about these topics.

Minimum Action Payload

Do you recall the action from a previous chapter that added a todo item? It was something like the following:

Code Playground

```
{
  type: 'TODO_ADD',
  todo: { id: '0', name: 'learn redux', completed: false },
}
```

As you can see, the `completed` property is defined as false boolean. In addition, you saw that the action and reducer from the previous chapter did work under these circumstances. However, a rule of thumb in Redux is to keep the action payload to a minimum.

In the example, when you want to add a todo in a Todo application, it would need at least the unique identifier and a name of a todo. But the `completed` property is unnecessary. The assumption is that every todo that is added to the store will be incomplete in the beginning. It wouldn't make sense in a Todo application to add completed todos, would it? Therefore, not the action would take care of the `completed` property but the reducer.

Instead of simply passing the whole todo object from the action into the list of todos in your reducer function:

Code Playground

```
function applyAddTodo(state, action) {
  return state.concat(action.todo);
}
```

You can add the `completed` property as hardcoded property to your reducer function:

Code Playground

```
function applyAddTodo(state, action) {
  const todo = Object.assign({}, action.todo, { completed: false });
  return state.concat(todo);
}
```

Finally, you can omit it in the action's payload:

Code Playground

```
{
  type: 'TODO_ADD',
  todo: { id: '0', name: 'learn redux' },
}
```

Now, you only defined the necessary payload in the action to add a todo item to the list in the store. Nevertheless, if at some point the Todo application decides to add uncompleted todos in the first place, you can add it in the action again and leave it out of the reducer. Ultimately, keeping the payload in the action to a minimum should be a best practice in Redux.

Action Type

Actions get evaluated in reducers by action type. The action type is the glue between both parts even though actions and reducers can be defined independently. To make the application more robust, you should extract the action type as a variable. Otherwise, you can run into typos where an action never reaches a reducer because you misspelled it.

Code Playground

```
const TODO_ADD = 'TODO_ADD';
const TODO_TOGGLE = 'TODO_TOGGLE';

const action = {
  type: TODO_ADD,
  todo: { id: '0', name: 'learn redux' },
};

const toggleTodoAction = {
  type: TODO_TOGGLE,
  todo: { id: '0' },
};
```

```
function reducer(state, action) {
  switch(action.type) {
    case TODO_ADD : {
      return applyAddTodo(state, action);
    }
    case TODO_TOGGLE : {
      return applyToggleTodo(state, action);
    }
    default : return state;
  }
}
```

There is another benefit in extracting the action type as variable. Because action, reducer and action type are loosely coupled, you can define them in separate files. You would only need to import the action type to use them only in specific actions and reducers. After all, action types could be used in multiple reducers too. This use case will be covered in another chapter when it comes to the advanced reducers.

Action Creator

Action creators add another layer on top, which often leads to confusion when learning Redux. Action creators are not mandatory, but they are convenient to use. So far, you have dispatched an action as plain action object:

Code Playground

```
const TODO_ADD = 'TODO_ADD';

store.dispatch({
  type: TODO_ADD,
  todo: { id: '0', name: 'learn redux' },
});
```

Action creators encapsulate the action with its action type and optional payload in a reusable function. By having a function for your action, you gain the flexibility to pass any payload to the action as arguments. After all, they are only pure functions which return an object.

Code Playground

```
function doAddTodo(id, name) {
  return {
    type: TODO_ADD,
    todo: { id, name },
  };
}
```

Now, you can use the action creator by invoking it as function in your dispatch method:

Code Playground

```
store.dispatch(doAddTodo('0', 'learn redux'));
```

Action creators return a plain action (object). Once again, it is not mandatory to use them, but it adds convenience and makes your code more readable in the long run. In addition, you can test action creators independently as functions. Last but not least, these action creators stay reusable because they are functions.

Optional Payload

In the book, it was mentioned earlier that actions don't need to have a payload. Only the action type is required. For instance, imagine you want to login into your Todo application. Therefore, you need to open up a modal where you can enter your credentials: email and password. You wouldn't need a payload for your action in order to open a modal. You only need to signalize that the modal state should be stored as "open" by dispatching an action.

Code Playground

```
{
  type: 'LOGIN_MODAL_OPEN',
}
```

A reducer would take care of it and set the state of a `isLoginModalOpen` boolean to true. While it is good to know that the payload is not mandatory in actions, the last example can lead to a bad practice. It is because you may already know that you would need a second action to close the modal again:

Code Playground

```
{
  type: 'LOGIN_MODAL_CLOSE',
}
```

Again a reducer would set the isLoginModalOpen boolean in the state to false. That's verbose, because you already need two actions to alter only one property in the state. By planning your actions thoughtfully, you avoid these bad practices and keep your actions on a higher level of abstraction. If you used the optional payload for the action, you could solve login scenario in only one action instead of two actions. The isLoginModalOpen property would be dynamically passed in the action rather than being hardcoded in a reducer.

Code Playground

```
{
  type: 'LOGIN_MODAL_TOGGLE',
  isLoginModalOpen: true,
}
```

By using an action creator, the payload can be passed in as arguments and thus stays flexible. Afterward, only one action instead of two is needed.

Code Playground

```
function doToggleLoginModal(open) {
  return {
    type: 'LOGIN_MODAL_TOGGLE',
    isLoginModalOpen: open,
  };
}
```

In Redux, actions should always try to stay on an abstract level rather than on a concrete level. Otherwise, you will end up with duplications and verbose actions. However, don't worry too much about it for now. This will be explained in more detail in another chapter in this book that is about commands and events.

Payload Structure

Again you will encounter a best practice that is not mandatory in Redux. So far, the payload was dumped without much thought in the actions. Now imagine an action that has a larger payload than a simple todo. For instance, the action payload should clarify to whom the todo is assigned.

Code Playground

```
{
  type: 'TODO_ADD_ASSIGNED',
  todo: { id: '0', name: 'learn redux' },
  assignedTo: { id: '99' name: 'Robin' },
}
```

The properties would add up horizontally in the object, but mask the one most important property, which is the action type, when they become too many. Therefore, you should treat action type and payload on the same level, but nest the payload itself one level deeper as the two abstract properties.

Code Playground

```
{
  type: 'TODO_ADD_ASSIGNED',
  payload: {
    todo: { id: '0', name: 'learn redux' },
    assignedTo: { id: '99' name: 'Robin' },
  },
}
```

The refactoring ensures that type and payload are visible on first glance. As said, it is not mandatory to do so and often adds more complexity. But in larger applications it keeps your action creators more readable.

Hands On: Redux Standalone with advanced Actions

Let's dip into the Redux Playground again with the acquired knowledge about actions. You can take the JS Bin project that you have done in the last chapter[52] again. The project will be used to show the advanced actions. You can try it on your own. Otherwise, the following part will guide you through the refactorings.

The minimum action payload is a quick refactoring. You can omit the `completed` property in the action and add it to the reducer functionality.

---

[52]https://jsbin.com/kopohur/28/edit?html,js,console

Code Playground

```
function applyAddTodo(state, action) {
  const todo = Object.assign({}, action.todo, { completed: false });
  return state.concat(todo);
}

...

store.dispatch({
  type: 'TODO_ADD',
  todo: { id: '0', name: 'learn redux' },
});

store.dispatch({
  type: 'TODO_ADD',
  todo: { id: '1', name: 'learn mobx' },
});
```

The next step is the extraction of the action types from the actions and reducer. They should be defined as variables and thus can be replaced in the reducer.

Code Playground

```
const TODO_ADD = 'TODO_ADD';
const TODO_TOGGLE = 'TODO_TOGGLE';

function reducer(state, action) {
  switch(action.type) {
    case TODO_ADD : {
      return applyAddTodo(state, action);
    }
    case TODO_TOGGLE : {
      return applyToggleTodo(state, action);
    }
    default : return state;
  }
}
```

In addition, you can use the variables in the dispatched actions too.

Code Playground

```
store.dispatch({
  type: TODO_ADD,
  todo: { id: '0', name: 'learn redux' },
});

store.dispatch({
  type: 'TODO_ADD',
  todo: { id: '1', name: 'learn mobx' },
});

store.dispatch({
  type: TODO_TOGGLE,
  todo: { id: '0' },
});
```

In the next step, you can introduce action creators to your Todo application. First, define them as functions:

Code Playground

```
function doAddTodo(id, name) {
  return {
    type: TODO_ADD,
    todo: { id, name },
  };
}

function doToggleTodo(id) {
  return {
    type: TODO_TOGGLE,
    todo: { id },
  };
}
```

And second, use them in your dispatch functions to return the action objects:

Code Playground

```
store.dispatch(doAddTodo('0', 'learn redux'));
store.dispatch(doAddTodo('1', 'learn mobx'));
store.dispatch(doToggleTodo('0'));
```

There were two more advanced topics about actions in this chapter: optional payload and payload structure. The first topic wouldn't apply in the current application. Every action has to have a payload in this scenario. The second topic could be applied. However, the payload is too small at this point in time and thus doesn't need to be restructured with an intermediate payload property.

The final Todo application can be found in this JS Bin[53]. You can do further experiments with it before you continue with the next chapter.

---

[53]https://jsbin.com/kopohur/29/edit?html,js,console

Advanced Reducers

Apart from the advanced topics about actions, there is more to know about reducers, too. Again, not everything is mandatory, but you should at least know about the following things to embrace best practices, common usage patterns and practices on scaling your state architecture.

Initial State

So far, you have provided your store with an initial state. It was an empty list of todos.

Code Playground

```
const store = createStore(reducer, []);
```

That's the initial state for the whole Redux store. However, you can apply the initial state on a more fine-grained level. Before you dispatch your first action, the Redux store will initialize by running through all reducers once. You can try it by removing all of your dispatches in the editor and add a `console.log()` in the reducer. You will see that it runs with an initializing action once, even though there is no dispatched action.

The initializing action, that is received in the reducer, is accompanied by the initial state that is specified in the `createStore()` function. However, if you leave out the initial state in the store initialization, the incoming state in the reducer will be `undefined`.

Code Playground

```
const store = createStore(reducer);
```

That's where you can opt-in to specify an initial state on a more fine-grained level. If the incoming state is `undefined`, you can default with a JavaScript ES6 default parameter[54] to a default initial state.

Code Playground

```
function reducer(state = [], action) {
  switch(action.type) {
    case TODO_ADD : {
      return applyAddTodo(state, action);
    }
    case TODO_TOGGLE : {
      return applyToggleTodo(state, action);
    }
    default : return state;
  }
}
```

---

[54]https://developer.mozilla.org/en/docs/Web/JavaScript/Reference/Functions/Default_parameters

The initial state will be the same as before, but you defined it on a more fine-grained level. Later on, that will help you when you specify more than one reducer and your state object becomes more complex because it it split up into multiple reducers. Then every reducer can define its fine-grained initial state.

Nested Data Structures

The initial state is an empty list of todos. However, in a growing application you want to operate on more than todos. You might have a currentUser object that represents the logged in user in your application. In addition, you want to have a filter property to filter todos by their completed property. In a growing application, more objects and arrays will gather in the global state. That's why your initial state shouldn't be an empty array but an object that represents the state object. This object then has nested properties for todos, currentUser and filter.

Disregarding the initial state in the reducer from the last chapter, you would define your initial state in the store like in the following:

Code Playground

```
const initialState = {
  todos: [],
};
const store = createStore(reducer, initialState);
```

Now you can use the space horizontally in your initialState object. It might grow to the following at some point:

Code Playground

```
const initialState = {
  currentUser: null,
  todos: [],
  filter: 'SHOW_ALL',
};
```

If you get back to your Todo application, you will have to adjust your reducer. The reducer deals with a list of todos as state, but now it is a complex global state object.

Code Playground

```
function reducer(state, action) {
  switch(action.type) {
    case TODO_ADD : {
      return applyAddTodo(state, action);
    }
    case TODO_TOGGLE : {
      return applyToggleTodo(state, action);
    }
    default : return state;
  }
}

function applyAddTodo(state, action) {
  const todo = Object.assign({}, action.todo, { completed: false });
  const todos = state.todos.concat(todo);
  return Object.assign({}, state, { todos });
}

function applyToggleTodo(state, action) {
  const todos = state.todos.map(todo =>
    todo.id === action.todo.id
      ? Object.assign({}, todo, { completed: !todo.completed })
      : todo
  );
  return Object.assign({}, state, { todos });
}
```

Those **nested data structures** are fine in Redux, but you want to avoid **deeply nested data structures**. As you can see, it adds complexity to create your new state object. Another chapter which you will read up later in the book will pick up this topic again. It will showcase how you can avoid deeply nested data structures by using a neat helper library with the name normalizr.

Combined Reducer

The next chapter is crucial to understand the principles of scaling state by using substates in Redux. In the previous chapters, you have heard about multiple reducers, but haven't used them yet. As you have learned, a reducer grows horizontally when it deals with more than one action type. But this doesn't scale at some point. You want to split your reducer up into two reducers or introduce another reducer right from the beginning. Imagine you had a reducer that served your todos, but you want to have a reducer for the `filter` state for your todos eventually. Another use case could be to have a reducer for the `currentUser` that is logged in into your Todo application.

You can already see a pattern on how to separate your reducers. It is usually by domain like todos, filter, or user. A todo reducer might be responsible to add, remove, edit and complete todos. A filter reducer is responsible to manage the filter state of your todos. A user reducer cares about user entities that could be the `currentUser` who is logged in in your application or a list of users who are assigned to todos. That's where you could again split up the user reducer to a `currentUser` reducer and a `assignedUsers` reducer. You can imagine how this approach, introducing reducers by domain, scales very well.

Let's enter **combined reducers** to enable you using multiple reducers. Redux gives you a helper to combine multiple reducers into one root reducer: `combineReducers()`. The function takes an object as argument which can have multiple reducers assigned to their state which they are going to manage.

Code Playground

```
const rootReducer = combineReducers({
  todoState: todoReducer,
  filterState: filterReducer,
});
```

Afterward, the `rootReducer` can be used to initialize the Redux store instead of the single todo reducer. After all, only one reducer is needed to initialize the Redux store. So it has to be a combination of multiple reducers when having more than one reducer.

Code Playground

```
const store = createStore(rootReducer);
```

That's it for the initialization of the Redux store with combined reducers. But what about the reducers themselves? There is already one reducer that cares about the todos, you would only have the rename it.

Code Playground

```
function todoReducer(state, action) {
  switch(action.type) {
    case TODO_ADD : {
      return applyAddTodo(state, action);
    }
    case TODO_TOGGLE : {
      return applyToggleTodo(state, action);
    }
    default : return state;
  }
}
```

The `filterReducer` is not there yet. It would look something like the following to set a filter for the todos (e.g. SHOW_ALL, SHOW_COMPLETED, SHOW_INCOMPLETED):

Code Playground

```
function filterReducer(state, action) {
  switch(action.type) {
    case FILTER_SET : {
      return applySetFilter(state, action);
    }
    default : return state;
  }
}
```

Now, there comes the important part: The `combineReducers()` function introduces an intermediate state layer for the global state object. The global state object, when using the combined reducers as shown before, would look like the following:

Code Playground

```
{
  todoState: ...,
  filterState: ...,
}
```

The property keys for the intermediate layer are those defined in the `combineReducers()` function. However, in your reducers the incoming state is not the global state object anymore. It is their defined substate from the `combinedReducers()` function. The `todoReducer` doesn't know anything about the `filterState` and the `filterReducer` doesn't know anything about the `todoState`.

The `filterReducer` and `todoReducer` can use the JavaScript ES6 default parameter to define their initial state.

Code Playground

```
function todoReducer(state = [], action) {
  switch(action.type) {
    case TODO_ADD : {
      return applyAddTodo(state, action);
    }
    case TODO_TOGGLE : {
      return applyToggleTodo(state, action);
    }
    default : return state;
  }
}

function filterReducer(state = 'SHOW_ALL', action) {
  switch(action.type) {
    case FILTER_SET : {
      return applySetFilter(state, action);
    }
    default : return state;
  }
}
```

Now your `apply` function in the reducers have to operate on these substates again.

Code Playground

```
function applyAddTodo(state, action) {
  const todo = Object.assign({}, action.todo, { completed: false });
  return state.concat(todo);
}

function applyToggleTodo(state, action) {
  return state.map(todo =>
    todo.id === action.todo.id
      ? Object.assign({}, todo, { completed: !todo.completed })
      : todo
  );
}

function applySetFilter(state, action) {
  return action.filter;
}
```

It seems like a lot of hassle to define multiple reducers and combining them eventually. But it is crucial knowledge to split up your global state into substates. These substates can be managed by their reducers who only operate on these substates. In addition, each reducer can be responsible to define the initial substate.

Clarification for Initial State

The last chapters moved around the initial state initialization from `createStore()` to the reducer(s) a few times. You might wonder where to initialize your state after all. Therefore, you have to distinguish whether you are using combined reducers or only one plain reducer.

One plain reducer: When using only one plain reducer, the initial state in `createStore()` dominates the initial state in the reducer. The initial state in the reducer only works when the incoming initial state is `undefined` because then it can apply the default state from the default parameter. But the initial state is already defined in `createStore()` and thus utilized by the reducer.

Combined reducers: When using combined reducers, you can embrace a more nuanced usage of the state initialization. The initial state object that is used for the `createStore()` function doesn't have to include all substates that are introduced by the `combineReducers()` function. Thus, when a substate is `undefined`, the reducer can define the default substate. Otherwise, the default substate from the `createStore()` is used.

Nested Reducers

By now, you know two things about scaling reducers in a growing application that demand sophisticated state management:

- a reducer can care about different action types
- a reducer can be split up into multiple reducers yet be combined as one root reducer for the store initialization

These steps are used to scale the reducers horizontally (even though combined reducers add at least one vertical level). A reducer operates on the global state or on a substate when using combined reducers. However, you can use nested reducers to introduce vertically levels of substate too.

Take for example the `todoReducer` that operates on a list of todos. From a technical perspective, a list of todos has single todo entities. So why not introduce a nested reducer that deals with the todo substate as entities?

Code Playground

```
function todoReducer(state = [], action) {
  switch(action.type) {
    case TODO_ADD : {
      return [ ...state, todoEntityReducer(undefined, action) ];
    }
    case TODO_TOGGLE : {
      return state.map(todo => todoEntityReducer(todo, action));
    }
    default : return state;
  }
}

function todoEntityReducer(state, action) {
  switch(action.type) {
    case TODO_ADD : {
      return applyAddTodo(state, action);
    }
    case TODO_TOGGLE : {
      return applyToggleTodo(state, action);
    }
    default : return state;
  }
}

function applyAddTodo(state, action) {
  return Object.assign({}, action.todo, { completed: false });
}

function applyToggleTodo(todo, action) {
  return todo.id === action.todo.id
    ? Object.assign({}, todo, { completed: !todo.completed })
    : todo
}
```

You can use nested reducers to introduce intermediate layers for substates. In addition, they can be reused. You might run into cases where you can reuse a nested reducer somewhere else. However, while nested reducers can give you a better picture on your state, they add more levels of complexity to your state, too. You should follow the practice of not nesting your state too deeply in the first place. Then you won't run into nested reducers often.

Hands On: Redux Standalone with advanced Reducers

Let's dip into the Redux Playground again with the acquired knowledge about reducers. Again, you can take the JS Bin project that you have done in the last chapter[55]. The project will be used to show the advanced reducers. You can try it on your own. Otherwise, the following part will guide you through the refactorings. First, let's add the second reducer to filter the todos.

Code Playground

```
const FILTER_SET = 'FILTER_SET';

function filterReducer(state = 'SHOW_ALL', action) {
  switch(action.type) {
    case FILTER_SET : {
      return applySetFilter(state, action);
    }
    default : return state;
  }
}

function applySetFilter(state, action) {
  return action.filter;
}
```

The reducer has an initial state. There is no action yet that serves the reducer though. You can add a simple action creator that only receives a string as argument for the filter property. You will experience later on, how this can be used in a real application.

Code Playground

```
function doSetFilter(filter) {
  return {
    type: FILTER_SET,
    filter,
  };
}
```

Second, you can rename your first reducer to todoReducer and give it an initial state of an empty list of todos.

---

[55]https://jsbin.com/kopohur/29/edit?html,js,console

Code Playground

```
function todoReducer(state = [], action) {
  switch(action.type) {
    case TODO_ADD : {
      return applyAddTodo(state, action);
    }
    case TODO_TOGGLE : {
      return applyToggleTodo(state, action);
    }
    default : return state;
  }
}
```

The initial state isn't initialized in the createStore() function anymore. It is initialized on a more fine-grained level in the reducers. When you recap the last lessons learned from the advanced reducers chapter, you will notice that you spared the back and forth with the initial state. Now, the todoReducer still operates on the todos substate and the new filterReducer operates on the filter substate. As third and last step, you have to combine both reducers to get this intermediate layer of substates in the first place. In the JS Bin you have Redux available as global variable to get the combineReducer function. Otherwise, you could import it with JavaScript ES6.

Code Playground

```
const rootReducer = Redux.combineReducers({
  todoState: todoReducer,
  filterState: filterReducer,
});
```

Now you can use the combined rootReducer in the store initialization.

Code Playground

```
const store = createStore(rootReducer);
```

When you run your application again, everything should work. You can now use the filterReducer as well.

Code Playground

```
store.dispatch(doAddTodo('0', 'learn redux'));
store.dispatch(doAddTodo('1', 'learn mobx'));
store.dispatch(doToggleTodo('0'));
store.dispatch(doSetFilter('COMPLETED'));
```

The Todo application favors initial state in reducers over initial state in createStore(). In addition, it will not use a nested todoEntityReducer for the sake of keeping the reducer hierarchy simple. Even though there is one intermediate state layer because of the combined reducers now.

The final Todo application can be found in this JS Bin[56]. You can do further experiments with it before continuing with the next chapter.

---

[56]https://jsbin.com/kopohur/30/edit?html,js,console

Redux in React

In the last chapters, you got to know plain Redux. It helps you to manage a predictable state object. However, you want to use this state object in an application eventually. It can be any JavaScript application that has to deal with state management. After all, the principle of Redux could be deployed to any programming language to manage a state object.

State management in single page applications (SPAs) is one of these use cases where Redux can be applied. These applications are usually built with a framework (Angular) or view layer library (React, Vue), but most often these solutions lack of a sophisticated state management. That's where Redux comes into play. The book focuses on React, but you can apply the learnings to other solutions, such as Angular and Vue, too.

The following scenarios could live without Redux, because they wouldn't run into state management issues with using only local state in the first place. But for the sake of demonstrating Redux in React, they will omit local state management and apply sophisticated state management with Redux.

Connecting the State

On the one hand you have React as your view layer. It has everything you need to build a component hierarchy. You can compose components into each other. In addition, the component's methods make sure that you always have a hook into their lifecycle.

On the other hand you have Redux. By now, you should know how to manage state in Redux. First, you initialize everything by setting up reducer(s), actions and their optional action creators. Afterward, the (combined) reducer is used to create the Redux store. Second, you can interact with the store by dispatching actions with plain action objects or with action creators, by subscribing to the store and by getting the current state from the store.

In the end, these three interactions need to be accessed from your view layer. As mentioned, the view layer can be anything, but to keep it focused, it will be React in this book.

If you recall the unidirectional data flow in Redux, that was adapted from the Flux architecture, you will notice that you have all parts at your disposal by now.

Concept Playground

```
View -> Action -> Reducer(s) -> Store -> View
```

How can dispatch(), subscribe() and getState() be accessed in a React View? Basically, the view layer has to be able to dispatch actions on the one end, while it has to listen to updates from the store, and get its state, in order to update itself, on the other end. All three functionalities are accessible as methods on the Redux store.

Hands On: Bootstrap React App with Redux

It is highly recommended to use create-react-app to bootstrap your React application. However, it is up to you to follow this advice. If you use create-react-app and have never used it before, you have to install it first from the command line by using the node package manager (npm):

Command Line

```
npm install -g create-react-app
```

Now you can bootstrap your React application with create-react-app, navigate into the folder, and start it·

Command Line

```
create-react-app taming-the-state-todo-app
cd taming-the-state-todo-app
npm start
```

If you haven't used create-react-app before, I recommend you to read up the basics in their official documentation[57]. Basically, your *src/* folder has several files. You will not use the *src/App.js* file in this application, but only the *src/index.js* file. Open up your editor and adjust your *src/index.js* file to the following:

src/index.js

```
import React from 'react';
import ReactDOM from 'react-dom';
import './index.css';

function TodoApp() {
  return <div>Todo App</div>;
}

ReactDOM.render(<TodoApp />, document.getElementById('root'));
```

Now, when you start your application again with `npm start`, you should see the displayed "Todo App" from the `TodoApp` component. Before you continue to build a React application now, let's hook in all of the Redux code that you have written in the previous chapters. First, install Redux in your project:

Command Line: /

```
npm install --save redux
```

Second, re-use the Redux code from the previous chapters in your *src/index.js* file. You start at the top to import the two Redux functionalities that you have used so far. They belong next to the imports that are already there:

---

[57]https://github.com/facebookincubator/create-react-app

src/index.js

```
import React from 'react';
import ReactDOM from 'react-dom';
import { combineReducers, createStore } from 'redux';
import './index.css';
```

Now, in between of your imports and your React code, you introduce your Redux functionalities. First, the action types:

src/index.js

```
// action types

const TODO_ADD = 'TODO_ADD';
const TODO_TOGGLE = 'TODO_TOGGLE';
const FILTER_SET = 'FILTER_SET';
```

Second, the reducers with their initial state:

src/index.js

```
// reducers

const todos = [
  { id: '0', name: 'learn redux' },
  { id: '1', name: 'learn mobx' },
];

function todoReducer(state = todos, action) {
  switch(action.type) {
    case TODO_ADD : {
      return applyAddTodo(state, action);
    }
    case TODO_TOGGLE : {
      return applyToggleTodo(state, action);
    }
    default : return state;
  }
}

function applyAddTodo(state, action) {
  const todo = Object.assign({}, action.todo, { completed: false });
```

```
    return state.concat(todo);
}

function applyToggleTodo(state, action) {
  return state.map(todo =>
    todo.id === action.todo.id
      ? Object.assign({}, todo, { completed: !todo.completed })
      : todo
  );
}

function filterReducer(state = 'SHOW_ALL', action) {
  switch(action.type) {
    case FILTER_SET : {
      return applySetFilter(state, action);
    }
    default : return state;
  }
}

function applySetFilter(state, action) {
  return action.filter;
}
```

Third, the action creators:

src/index.js

```
// action creators

function doAddTodo(id, name) {
  return {
    type: TODO_ADD,
    todo: { id, name },
  };
}

function doToggleTodo(id) {
  return {
    type: TODO_TOGGLE,
    todo: { id },
  };
}
```

```
function doSetFilter(filter) {
  return {
    type: FILTER_SET,
    filter,
  };
}
```

And last but not least, the creation of the store with both reducers as one combined reducer:

src/index.js

```
// store

const rootReducer = combineReducers({
  todoState: todoReducer,
  filterState: filterReducer,
});

const store = createStore(rootReducer);
```

After that, your React code follows. It should already be there in the same file.

src/index.js

```
// view layer

function TodoApp() {
  return <div>Todo App</div>;
}

ReactDOM.render(<TodoApp />, document.getElementById('root'));
```

The React and Redux setup is done. This application can be found in a GitHub repository[58]. Now you have a running React application and a Redux store. But they don't work together yet. The next step is to wire both together.

---

[58]https://github.com/rwieruch/taming-the-state-todo-app/tree/0.0.0

Hands On: Naive Todo with React and Redux

The following will showcase a naive scenario of combining Redux in React. So far, you only have a TodoApp component in React. However, you want to start a component tree that can display a list of todos and gives the user the possibility to toggle these todos to a completed status. Apart from the TodoApp component, you will have a TodoList component and a TodoItem component. The TodoItem shows the name of the todo and has a functionality that is used in a button to complete the todo.

First, the TodoApp component:

src/index.js

```
function TodoApp({ todos, onToggleTodo }) {
  return <TodoList
    todos={todos}
    onToggleTodo={onToggleTodo}
  />;
}
```

Second, the TodoList component:

src/index.js

```
function TodoList({ todos, onToggleTodo }) {
  return (
    <div>
      {todos.map(todo => <TodoItem
        key={todo.id}
        todo={todo}
        onToggleTodo={onToggleTodo}
      />)}
    </div>
  );
}
```

Third, the TodoItem component:

src/index.js

```
function TodoItem({ todo, onToggleTodo }) {
  const { name, id, completed } = todo;
  return (
    <div>
      {name}
      <button
        type="button"
        onClick={() => onToggleTodo(id)}
      >
        {completed ? "Incomplete" : "Complete"}
      </button>
    </div>
  );
}
```

Notice that none of these components is aware of Redux. They simply display todos and use a callback function to toggle todo items to either complete or incomplete. Now, in the last step, you wire together Redux and React. You can use the created Redux store instance in your React root component where React hooks into HTML.

src/index.js

```
ReactDOM.render(
  <TodoApp
    todos={store.getState().todoState}
    onToggleTodo={id => store.dispatch(doToggleTodo(id))}
  />,
  document.getElementById('root')
);
```

The store does two things: it makes state accessible and exposes functionalities to alter the state. The todos props are passed down to the TodoApp by retrieving them from the Redux store instance. In addition, a onToggleTodo property is passed down which is a function. This function is a higher-order function that wraps the dispatching of an action that is created by its action creator. However, the TodoApp component is completely unaware of the todos being retrieved from the Redux store or of the onToggleTodo() being a dispatched action on the Redux store. These passed properties are props for the TodoApp. You can start your application again with npm start and see the todos displayed but not updated yet after clicking the button.

So what about the update mechanism? When an action is dispatched, someone needs to subscribe to the Redux store. In a naive approach, you can do the following to force a view update in React. First, wrap your React root component into a function.

src/index.js

```
function render() {
  ReactDOM.render(
    <TodoApp
      todos={store.getState().todoState}
      onToggleTodo={id => store.dispatch(doToggleTodo(id))}
    />,
    document.getElementById('root')
  );
}
```

Second, you can pass the function to the subscribe() method of the Redux store as callback function. This way, the function is every time called when the state in the Redux store changes. And last but not least, you have to invoke the function one time on your own for the initial rendering of your React component.

src/index.js

```
function render() {
  ReactDOM.render(
    <TodoApp
      todos={store.getState().todoState}
      onToggleTodo={id => store.dispatch(doToggleTodo(id))}
    />,
    document.getElementById('root')
  );
}

store.subscribe(render);
render();
```

The Todo application should display the todos and update the completed state once you toggle it. The final application of this approach can be found in a GitHub repository[59].

The approach showcased how you can wire up your React component tree with the Redux store. The components don't need to be aware of the Redux store at all, but the React root component is. In addition, everything is forcefully re-rendered when the global state in the Redux store updates, because the render function called on every state change.

Even though the previous approach is pragmatic and shows a simplified version of how to wire up all these things, it is a naive approach of doing it. Why is that? In a real application you want to avoid the following bad practices:

---

[59]https://github.com/rwieruch/taming-the-state-todo-app/tree/1.0.1

- re-rendering every component: You want to re-render only the components that are affected by the global state updated in the Redux store. Otherwise, you will run into performance issues in a larger application, because every component needs to render again.
- using the store instance directly: You want to avoid to operate directly on the Redux store instance. The store should be injected somehow into your React component tree to make it accessible for components that need to have access to the store.
- making the store globally available: The store shouldn't be globally accessible by every component. In the previous example only the React root component uses it, but who prevents you from using (importing) it directly in your TodoItem component to dispatch an action?

Fortunately, there exists a library that takes care of these things and gives you a bridge from the Redux to the React world. It connects your state layer with your view layer and clearly separates both constraints.

Connecting the State, but Sophisticated

A library called react-redux[60] gives you two things in order to wire up Redux with React. First, it gives you a `<Provider />` component. When using Redux with React, the `Provider` component should be the top level component of your application. The component has one prop as input: the Redux store that you created with `createStore()`.

Code Playground

```
import { Provider } from 'react-redux'

ReactDOM.render(
  <Provider store={store}>
    <App />
  </Provider>,
  document.getElementById('root')
);
```

After you have done this, every child component in the whole component tree has implicit access to the store. Thus, every component is able to dispatch actions and to listen to updates in order to re-render. But not every component has to listen to updates. How does this work without passing the store as prop to each child component? It uses the provider pattern that you got to know in a previous chapter when only doing state management with React. Under the hood, it uses the React context API:

"In some cases, you want to pass data through the component tree without having to pass the props down manually at every level. You can do this directly in React with the powerful "context" API."

That was part one to use Redux in React. Second, you can use a higher-order component that is called `connect` from the new library. It makes the Redux store functionality dispatch and the state from the store itself available to the components that are enhanced by this higher-order component.

Code Playground

```
import { connect } from 'react-redux'

function Component(props) {
  ...
}

const ConnectedComponent = connect(...)(Component);
```

The connect HOC can have up to four arguments as configuration:

---

[60]https://github.com/reactjs/react-redux

Code Playground

```
connect([mapStateToProps], [mapDispatchToProps], [mergeProps], [options])(...);
```

Usually, you will only use two of them: mapStateToProps() and mapDispatchToProps(). You will learn about the other two arguments, mergeProps() and options, later in this book.

mapStateToProps(state, [props]) ⇒ derivedProps: It is a function that can be passed to the connect HOC. If it is passed, the input component of the connect HOC will subscribe to updates from the Redux store. Thus, it means that every time the store subscription notices an update, the mapStateToProps() function will run. The mapStateToProps() function itself has two arguments in its function signature: the global state object from the provided Redux store and optionally the props from the parent component where the enhanced component is used eventually. After all, the function returns an object that is derived from the global state and optionally from the props from the parent component. The returned object will be merged into the remaining props that come as input from the parent component.

mapDispatchToProps(dispatch, [props]): It is a function (or object) that can be passed to the connect HOC. Whereas mapStateToProps() gives access to the global state, mapDispatchToProps() gives access to the dispatch method of the Redux store. It makes it possible to dispatch actions but passes down only plain functions that wire up the dispatching in a higher-order function. After all, it makes it possible to pass functions down to the input component of the connect HOC to alter the state. Optionally, here you can also use the incoming props to wrap those into the dispatched action.

That is a lot of knowledge to digest. Both functions, mapStateToProps() and mapDispatchToProps(), can be intimidating at the beginning. In addition, they are used in a higher-order component. However, they only give you access to the state and the dispatch method of the Redux store.

Concept Playground

```
View -> (mapDispatchToProps) -> Action -> Reducer(s) -> Store -> (mapStateToProp\
s) -> View
```

You will see in the following examples that these functions don't need to be intimidating at all. They are your common tools to connect the state layer with your view layer on both ends.

Hands On: Sophisticated Todo with React and Redux

Now you will use react-redux to wire up React with Redux. Let's get back to your Todo Application from a previous chapter. First, you have to install the new library in order to connect both worlds:

Command Line: /

```
npm install --save react-redux
```

Second, instead of wrapping the React root component into the render() function and subscribing it to the store.subscribe() method, you will use the plain React root component again but use the Provider component given by react-redux.

src/index.js

```
import React from 'react';
import ReactDOM from 'react-dom';
import { combineReducers, createStore } from 'redux';
import { Provider } from 'react-redux';
import './index.css';

...

ReactDOM.render(
  <Provider store={store}>
    <TodoApp />
  </Provider>,
  document.getElementById('root')
);
```

It uses the plain TodoApp component. The component still expects todos and onToggleTodo as props. But it doesn't have these props. Let's use the connect higher-order component to expose these to the TodoApp component. The TodoApp component will become a connected TodoApp component.

src/index.js

```
import React from 'react';
import ReactDOM from 'react-dom';
import { combineReducers, createStore } from 'redux';
import { Provider, connect } from 'react-redux';
import './index.css';

...

const ConnectedTodoApp = connect(mapStateToProps, mapDispatchToProps)(TodoApp);

ReactDOM.render(
  <Provider store={store}>
```

```
    <ConnectedTodoApp />
  </Provider>,
  document.getElementById('root')
);
```

Now, only the connections, mapStateToProps() and mapDispatchToProps() are missing. They are quite similar to the naive React with Redux version.

src/index.js

```
function mapStateToProps(state) {
  return {
    todos: state.todoState,
  };
}

function mapDispatchToProps(dispatch) {
  return {
    onToggleTodo: id => dispatch(doToggleTodo(id)),
  };
}

const ConnectedTodoApp = connect(mapStateToProps, mapDispatchToProps)(TodoApp);
```

. . .

That's it. In mapStateToProps() only a substate is returned. In mapDispatchToProps() only a higher-order function that encapsulates the dispatching of an action is returned. The child components are unaware of any state or actions. They are only receiving props. In this case, the props are todos and onToggleTodo. The final application of this approach can be found in a GitHub repository[61]. I would advice you to compare it to the naive version again that wires React and Redux together. It is not that different from it.

Hands On: Connecting State Everywhere

There is one last clue to understand the basics of wiring React and Redux together. In the previous example, you only used one connected component that is located at the root of your component tree. But you can use connected components everywhere. So let's experience it with in a real use case in your Todo application.

---

[61]https://github.com/rwieruch/taming-the-state-todo-app/tree/2.0.0

Use case: Only your TodoApp component has access to the state and enables you to alter the state. Instead of using your root component to connect to it to the store, you can add connected components everywhere in your React component tree. For instance, the onToggleTodo() function has to pass several components until it reaches its destination in the TodoItem component. Why not connecting the TodoItem component to make the functionality right next to it available rather than passing it down to multiple components which are not interested in it? The same applies for the TodoList component. It could be connected to retrieve the list of todos instead of getting it from the TodoApp component which doesn't care about the list.

In the Todo application, you could keep both mapStateToProps() and mapDispatchToProps(), there business logic stays the same, but you would use them somewhere else in your React component tree. While the TodoApp component doesn't need them anymore, they would be used in a connected TodoItem and connected TodoList component.

src/index.js

```
const ConnectedTodoList = connect(mapStateToProps)(TodoList);
const ConnectedTodoItem = connect(null, mapDispatchToProps)(TodoItem);

ReactDOM.render(
  <Provider store={store}>
    <TodoApp />
  </Provider>,
  document.getElementById('root')
);
```

Now you wouldn't need to pass the onToggleTodo() props through the TodoApp component and TodoList component anymore. The same applies for the todos that don't need to get passed through the TodoApp component.

src/index.js

```
function TodoApp() {
  return <ConnectedTodoList />;
}

function TodoList({ todos }) {
  return (
    <div>
      {todos.map(todo => <ConnectedTodoItem
        key={todo.id}
        todo={todo}
      />)}
    </div>
```

```
    );
}
```

The final Todo application can be found in the GitHub repository[62].

As you can imagine by now, you can connect your state everywhere to your view layer. You can retrieve it with mapStateToProps() and alter it with mapDispatchToProps() from everywhere in your component tree. These components that add this intermediate glue between view and state are called connected components. They are a subset of the container components from the container and presenter pattern, whereas the presenter components are still clueless and don't know if the props are derived from a Redux store, from local state or actions. They just use these props.

After all, that's basically everything you need to connect your state layer (Redux) to a view layer (React). As mentioned, your view layer could be implemented with another library such as Vue as well.

---

[62]https://github.com/rwieruch/taming-the-state-todo-app/tree/3.0.0

Redux State Structure and Retrieval

In the previous chapters, you have learned about Redux standalone and Redux in React. You would already be able to build smaller and medium sized applications with it. Before you dive deeper into Redux, I recommend you to experiment with your recent learnings and apply them in your applications. If you jump straight into the next chapters, you may get the feeling that Redux is overkill (which it is for most of the applications out there). However, the coming chapters should give you advanced guidance when scaling your state management with Redux in larger applications. There are a couple of techniques you can apply then.

The following chapter guides you through more advanced topics in Redux to manage your state. You will get to know the middleware in Redux, you will learn more about a normalized and immutable state structure, and how to retrieve a substate in an improved way from the global state with selectors.

Middleware in Redux

In Redux, you can use a middleware. Every dispatched action in Redux flows through this middleware. You can opt-in a specific feature in between of dispatching an action and the moment it reaches the reducer.

There are useful libraries out there to opt-in features into your Redux middleware. In the following, you will get to know one of them: redux-logger[63]. When you use it, it doesn't change anything in your application. But it will make your life easier as developer when dealing with Redux. What does it do? It simply logs the actions in your browser's developer console with console.log(). As a developer, it gives you clarity on which action is dispatched and how the previous and the new state are structured.

But where to apply this middleware in Redux? It is the Redux store which can be initialized with it. The createStore() functionality from Redux takes as third argument a so called enhancer. The redux library comes with one of these enhancers: applyMiddleware().

Code Playground

```
import { applyMiddleware, createStore } from 'redux';

const store = createStore(
  reducer,
  undefined,
  applyMiddleware(...)
);
```

If you don't have an initial state for your Redux state, you can use undefined for it. Now, when using redux-logger, you can pass a logger instance to the applyMiddleware() function.

Code Playground

```
import { applyMiddleware, createStore } from 'redux';
import { createLogger } from 'redux-logger';

const logger = createLogger();

const store = createStore(
  reducer,
  undefined,
  applyMiddleware(logger)
);
```

---

[63]https://github.com/evgenyrodionov/redux-logger

That's it. Now every action should be visible in your browser's developer console when dispatching them. And thus your state changes become more predictable as developer without logging every action yourself.

The `applyMiddleware()` functionality takes any number of middleware: `applyMiddleware(firstMiddleware, secondMiddleware, ...)`;. The action will flow through all middleware before it reaches the reducers. Sometimes, you have to make sure to apply them in the correct order. For instance, the `redux-logger` middleware must be last in the middleware chain in order to output the correct actions and states.

Nevertheless, that's only the redux-logger middleware. On your way to implement Redux applications, you will surely find out more about useful features that can be applied with the Redux middleware. Most of these features are already taken care of in libraries that you will find published with npm. For instance, asynchronous actions in Redux are possible by using the Redux middleware. These asynchronous actions will be explained later in this book.

Immutable State

Redux embraces an immutable state. Your reducers will always return a new state object. You will never mutate the incoming state. Therefore, you might have to get used to different JavaScript functionalities and syntax to embrace immutable data structures.

So far, you have used built-in JavaScript functionalities to keep your data structures immutable. Such as `array.map()` and `array.concat(item)` for arrays or `Object.assign()` for objects. All of these functionalities return new instances of arrays or objects without altering the old arrays and objects. Often, you have to read the official JavaScript documentation to make sure that they return a new instance of the array or object. Otherwise, you would violate the constraints of Redux because you would mutate the previous instance which in this case is often the state or action.

But it doesn't end here. You should know about your tools to keep data structures immutable in JavaScript. There are a handful of third-party libraries that can support you in keeping them immutable.

- immutable.js[64]
- immer.js[65]
- mori.js[66]
- seamless-immutable.js[67]
- baobab.js[68]

But all of them come with three drawbacks. First, they add another layer of complexity to your application. Second, you have to learn yet another library. And third, you have to dehydrate and rehydrate your data, because most of these libraries wrap your vanilla JavaScript objects and arrays into a library specific immutable data object and array. It is an immutable data object/array in your Redux store, but once you want to use it in React you have to transform it into a plain JavaScript object/array. Personally I would recommend to use such libraries only in two scenarios:

- You are not comfortable to keep your data structures immutable with JavaScript ES5, JavaScript ES6 and beyond.
- You want to improve the performance of immutable data structures when using huge amounts of data.

If both statements are false, I would highly recommend you to stick to plain JavaScript. As you have seen, the built-in JavaScript functionalities already help a lot for keeping data structures immutable.

---

[64]https://github.com/facebook/immutable-js

[65]https://github.com/mweststrate/immer

[66]https://github.com/swannodette/mori

[67]https://github.com/rtfeldman/seamless-immutable

[68]https://github.com/Yomguithereal/baobab

In JavaScript ES6 and beyond you get one more functionality to keep your data structures immutable: spread operators[69]. Spreading an object or array into a new object or new array always gives you a new object or new array.

Do you recall how you added a new todo item or how you completed a todo item in your reducers?

Code Playground

```
// adding todo
const todo = Object.assign({}, action.todo, { completed: false });
const newTodos = todos.concat(todo);

// toggling todo
const newTodos = todos.map(todo =>
  todo.id === action.todo.id
    ? Object.assign({}, todo, { completed: !todo.completed })
    : todo
  );
```

If you added more JavaScript ES6 by using the spread operator, you can keep these even more concise.

Code Playground

```
// adding todo
const todo = { ...action.todo, completed: false };
const newTodos = [ ...todos, todo ];

// toggling todo
const newTodos = todos.map(todo =>
  todo.id === action.todo.id
    ? { ...todo, completed: !todo.completed }
    : todo
  );
```

JavaScript gives you enough tools to keep your data structures immutable. There is no need to use a third-party library except for the two mentioned use cases. However, there might be a third use case where such library would help: deeply nested data structures in Redux that need to be kept immutable. It is true that it becomes more difficult to keep data structures immutable when they are nested. But, as mentioned earlier in the book, it is bad practice to have deeply nested data structures in Redux in the first place. That's where the next chapter of the book comes into play that can be used to keep your data structures flat in the Redux store.

---

[69]https://developer.mozilla.org/en/docs/Web/JavaScript/Reference/Operators/Spread_operator

Normalized State

A best practice in Redux is a flat state structure. You don't want to maintain an immutable structure for your state when it is deeply nested. It becomes tedious and unreadable even with spread operators. But often you don't have control over your data structure, because it comes from a backend application by using its API. When having a deeply nested data structure, you have two options:

- saving it in the store as it is and postpone the problem (not good)
- saving it as normalized data structure in the store (good)

You should try to default to the second option. You only deal with the problem once and all subsequent parts in your application will be grateful for it. Let's run through one scenario to illustrate the normalization of data. Imagine you have the following nested data structure:

Code Playground

```
const todos = [
  {
    id: '0',
    name: 'create redux',
    completed: true,
    assignedTo: {
      id: '99',
      name: 'Dan Abramov',
    },
  },
  {
    id: '1',
    name: 'create mobx',
    completed: true,
    assignedTo: {
      id: '77',
      name: 'Michel Weststrate',
    },
  }
];
```

Both library creators, Dan Abramov and Michel Weststrate, did a great job: they created popular libraries for state management. The first option, as mentioned, would be to save the todos as they are in the store. The todos themselves would have the deeply nested information of the `assignedTo` object within the `todo` object. Now, if an action wanted to correct an assigned user, the reducer would have to deal with the deeply nested data structure. Let's add Andrew Clark as creator of Redux.

Code Playground

```
const ASSIGNED_TO_CHANGE = 'ASSIGNED_TO_CHANGE';

store.dispatch({
  type: ASSIGNED_TO_CHANGE,
  payload: {
    todoId: '0',
    name: 'Dan Abramov and Andrew Clark',
  },
});

function todoReducer(state = [], action) {
  switch(action.type) {
    case ASSIGNED_TO_CHANGE : {
      return applyChangeAssignedTo(state, action);
    }

    ...

    default : return state;
  }
}

function applyChangeAssignedTo(state, action) {
  return state.map(todo => {
    if (todo.id === action.payload.todoId) {
      const assignedTo = { ...todo.assignedTo, name: action.payload.name };
      return { ...todo, assignedTo };
    } else {
      return todo;
    }
  });
}
```

This would lead to the following list of todos in your Redux store after the action has been dispatched:

Code Playground

```
const todos = [
  {
    id: '0',
    name: 'create redux',
    completed: true,
    assignedTo: {
      id: '99',
      name: 'Dan Abramov and Andrew Clark',
    },
  },
  {
    id: '1',
    name: 'create mobx',
    completed: true,
    assignedTo: {
      id: '77',
      name: 'Michel Weststrate',
    },
  }
];
```

As you can see from the reducer, the further you have to reach into a deeply nested data structure, the more you have to be careful to keep your data structure immutable. Each level of nested data adds more tedious work of maintaining it. Therefore, you could use a library called normalizr[70] to flatten (normalize) your state. The library uses schema definitions to transform deeply nested data structures into dictionaries that have entities and a corresponding list of ids.

What would that look like? Let's take the previous list of todo items as example. First, you would have to define schemas for your entities only once:

Code Playground

```
import { schema } from 'normalizr';

const assignedToSchema = new schema.Entity('assignedTo');

const todoSchema = new schema.Entity('todo', {
  assignedTo: assignedToSchema,
});
```

Second, you can normalize your data whenever you want:

---

[70]https://github.com/paularmstrong/normalizr

Code Playground

```
import { schema, normalize } from 'normalizr';

const assignedToSchema = new schema.Entity('assignedTo');

const todoSchema = new schema.Entity('todo', {
  assignedTo: assignedToSchema,
});

const normalizedData = normalize(todos, [ todoSchema ]);
```

The output would be the following:

Code Playground

```
{
  entities: {
    assignedTo: {
      77: {
        id: "77",
        name: "Michel Weststrate"
      },
      99: {
        id: "99",
        name: "Dan Abramov"
      }
    },
    todo: {
      0: {
        assignedTo: "99",
        completed: true,
        id: "0",
        name: "create redux"
      },
      1: {
        assignedTo: "77",
        completed: true,
        id: "1",
        name: "create mobx"
      }
    }
  },
```

```
  result: ["0", "1"]
}
```

The deeply nested data became a flat data structure grouped by entities. Each entity can reference another entity by its id. It is like you would keep these entities in a database. They are decoupled now. Afterward, in your Redux application, you could have one reducer that stores and deals with the assignedTo entities and one reducer that deals with the todo entities. The data structure is flat and grouped by entities and thus easier to access and to manipulate.

There is another benefit in normalizing your data. When your data is not normalized, entities are often duplicated in your nested data structure. Imagine the following object with todos.

Code Playground

```
const todos = [
  {
    id: '0',
    name: 'write a book',
    completed: true,
    assignedTo: {
      id: '55',
      name: 'Robin Wieruch',
    },
  },
  {
    id: '1',
    name: 'call it taming the state in react',
    completed: true,
    assignedTo: {
      id: '55',
      name: 'Robin Wieruch',
    },
  }
];
```

If you store such denormalized data in your Redux store, you will likely run into an major issue: Imagine you want to update the name property Robin Wieruch of all assignedTo properties. You would have to run through all todos in order to update all assignedTo properties with the id 55. The problem: There is no single source of truth. You will likely forget to update an entity and run into a stale state eventually. Therefore, the best practice is to store your state normalized so that each entity is a single source of truth. There will be no duplication of entities and thus no stale state when updating the one single source of truth, because each todo will reference to the updated assignedTo entity:

Code Playground

```
{
  entities: {
    assignedTo: {
      55: {
        id: "55",
        name: "Robin Wieruch"
      }
    },
    todo: {
      0: {
        assignedTo: "55",
        completed: true,
        id: "0",
        name: "write a book"
      },
      1: {
        assignedTo: "55",
        completed: true,
        id: "1",
        name: "call it taming the state in react"
      }
    }
  },
  result: ["0", "1"]
}
```

In conclusion, normalizing your state has two benefits. It keeps your state flat and thus easier manageable with immutable data structures. In addition, it groups entities to single sources of truth without any duplications. When you normalize your state, you will automatically get groupings of entities that could lead to their own reducers managing them. However, you don't want to start out with normalizing your state from the beginning. First you should try to introduce Redux itself to your application. Once you experience difficulties when altering your state, because it is deeply nested, or you experience issues updating single entities, because there is no single source of truth, you would want to introduce state normalization in your Redux application.

Before you will apply the normalization in your own Todo application as exercise, there exists yet another benefit when normalizing your state with a library such as normalizr. It is about denormalization: how do components retrieve the normalized state? You will learn it in the next chapter.

Selectors

In Redux, there is the concept of selectors to retrieve derived properties from your state. A selector is a function that takes the state as argument and returns a substate or derived properties of it. It can be that they only return a substate of your global state or that they already preprocess your state to return derived properties. The function can take optional arguments to support the selection process.

Plain Selectors

Selectors usually follow one syntax. The mandatory argument of a selector is the state from where it has to select from. There can be optional arguments that are in a supportive role to select the substate or the derived properties.

Code Playground

```
// selector
(state) => derived properties
// selector with optional arguments
(state, args) => derived properties
```

Selectors are not mandatory. When thinking about all the parts in Redux, only the action(s), the reducer(s) and the Redux store are a binding requirement. Similar to action creators, selectors can be used to achieve an improved developer experience in a Redux architecture, but you don't need to use them. What does a selector look like? It is a plain function, as mentioned, that could live anywhere in your application. However, you would use it, maybe import it, when using Redux in React, in your mapStateToProps() function. So instead of retrieving the state explicitly:

Code Playground

```
function mapStateToProps(state) {
  return {
    todos: state.todoState,
  };
}
```

You would retrieve it implicitly via a selector:

Code Playground

```
function getTodos(state) {
  return state.todoState;
}

function mapStateToProps(state) {
  return {
    todos: getTodos(state),
  };
}
```

It is similar to the action and reducer concept. Instead of manipulating the state directly in the Redux store, you will use action(s) and reducer(s) to alter it indirectly. The same applies for selectors that don't retrieve the derived properties directly but indirectly from the global state.

You may wonder: Why are selectors an advantage? There are several benefits. A selector can be reused. You will run into cases where you select the derived properties or substate more often from the global state. For instance, you may have multiple places in your application where you want to show only completed todo items. And that's always a good sign to use a function in the first place. In addition, selectors can be tested separately. They are pure functions and thus an easily testable part in your application and the overall Redux architecture. Last but not least, deriving properties from state can become a complex undertaking in a scaling application. As mentioned, a selector could get optional arguments to derive more sophisticated properties from the state. The selector function itself would become more complex, but it would be encapsulated in one function rather than, for instance in React and Redux, in multiple mapStateToProps() functions.

Denormalize State in Selectors

In the previous chapter about normalization, there was one benefit left unexplained. It is about selecting normalized state from your state layer to pass it to your view layer. Personally, I would argue a normalized state structure makes it much more convenient to select a substate from it. When you recall the normalized state structure, it looked something like the following:

Code Playground

```
{
  entities: ...
  ids: ...
}
```

For instance, in a real work application it would look like the following:

Code Playground

```
// state
[
  { id: '0', name: 'learn redux' },
  { id: '1', name: 'learn mobx' },
]

// normalized state
{
  entities: {
    0: {
      id: '0',
      name: 'learn redux',
    },
    1: {
      id: '1',
      name: 'learn redux',
    },
  },
  ids: ['0', '1'],
}
```

If you recall the Redux in React chapter, there you passed the list of todos from the `TodoList` component, because it is a connected component, down to the whole component tree. How would you solve this with the normalized state from above?

Assuming that the reducer stored the state in a normalized immutable data structure, you would only pass the list of todo `ids` to your `TodoList` component. Because this component manages the list and not the entities themselves, it makes perfect sense that it only gets the list with references to the entities.

Code Playground

```
function TodoList({ todosAsIds }) {
  return (
    <div>
      {todosAsIds.map(todoId => <ConnectedTodoItem
        key={todoId}
        todoId={todoId}
      />)}
    </div>
  );
```

```
}

function getTodosAsIds(state) {
  return state.todoState.ids;
}

function mapStateToProps(state) {
  return {
    todosAsIds: getTodosAsIds(state),
  };
}

const ConnectedTodoList = connect(mapStateToProps)(TodoList);
```

Now the ConnectedTodoItem component, that already passes the onToggleTodo() handler via the
mapDispatchToProps() function to its plain TodoItem component, would select the todo entity
matching to the incoming todoId property.

Code Playground

```
function getTodoAsEntity(state, id) {
  return state.todoState.entities[id];
}

function mapStateToProps(state, props) {
  return {
    todo: getTodoAsEntity(state, props.todoId),
  };
}

function mapDispatchToProps(dispatch) {
  return {
    onToggleTodo: id => dispatch(doToggleTodo(id)),
  };
}

const ConnectedTodoItem = connect(
  mapStateToProps,
  mapDispatchToProps
)(TodoItem);
```

The TodoItem component itself would stay the same. It still gets the todo item and the onTog-
gleTodo() handler as arguments. In addition, you can see two more concepts that were explained

earlier. First, the selector grows in complexity because it gets optional arguments to select derived properties from the state. Second, the mapStateToProps() function makes use of the incoming props from the TodoList component that uses the ConnectedTodoItem component.

As you can see, the normalized state requires to use more connected components. More components are responsible to select their needed derived properties. But in a growing application, following this pattern can make it easier to reason about it. You only pass properties that are really necessary to the component. In the last case, the TodoList component only cares about a list of references yet the TodoItem component itself cares about the entity that is selected by using the reference passed down by the TodoList component.

There exists another way to denormalize your normalized state when using a library such as normalizr. The previous scenario allowed you to only pass the minimum of properties to the components. Each component was responsible to select its state. In the nexy scenario, you will denormalize your state in one component while the other components don't need to care about it. You will use the defined schema, which you have used for the initial normalization, to reverse the normalization.

Code Playground

```
import { denormalize, schema } from 'normalizr';

const todoSchema = new schema.Entity('todos');
const todosSchema = { todos: [ todoSchema ] };

function TodoList({ todos }) {
  return (
    <div>
      {todos.map(todo => <ConnectedTodoItem
        key={todo.id}
        todo={todo}
      />)}
    </div>
  );
}

function getTodos(state) {
  const entities = state.todoState.entities;
  const ids = state.todoState.ids;
  return denormalize(ids, [ todoSchema ], entities);
}

function mapStateToProps(state) {
  return {
    todos: getTodos(state),
```

```
  };
}
```

```
const ConnectedTodoList = connect(mapStateToProps)(TodoList);
```

In this scenario, the whole normalized data structure gets denormalized in the selector. You will have the whole list of todos in your TodoList component. The TodoItem component wouldn't need to take care about the denormalization.

As you can see, there are two essential ways on how to deal with normnalized state in your selectors or in general in the mapStateToProps() functions. It is up to you to find about the best suited implementation for your own use case. Perhaps you even don't need to normalize your state in the first place, because it is already flat or not very deeply nested.

Reselect

When using selectors in a scaling application, you should consider a library called reselect[71] that provides you with advanced selectors. Basically, it uses the same concept of plain selectors as you have learned before, but comes with two improvements.

A plain selector has one constraint:

- *"Selectors can compute derived data, allowing Redux to store the minimal possible state."*

There are two more constraints when using selectors from the reselect library:

- *"Selectors are efficient. A selector is not recomputed unless one of its arguments change."*
- *"Selectors are composable. They can be used as input to other selectors."*

Selectors are pure functions without any side-effects. The output doesn't change when the input stays the same. Therefore, when a function is called twice and its arguments didn't change, it returns the same output. This proposition is used in reselect's selectors. It is called memoization in programming. A selector doesn't need to compute everything again when its input didn't change. It will simply return the same output, because it is a pure function. With memoization it remembers the previous input and if the input didn't change it returns the previous output. In a scaling application this can have a performance impacts.

Another benefit, when using reselect, is the ability to compose selectors. It supports the case of implementing reusable selectors that only solve one problem. Afterward they can be composed in a functional programming style.

---

[71]https://github.com/reactjs/reselect

The book will not dive deeper into the reselect library. When learning Redux it is good to know about these advanced selectors, but you are fine by using plain selectors in the beginning. If you cannot stay put, you can read up the example usages in the official GitHub repository[72] and apply in your projects while reading the book.

---

[72]https://github.com/reactjs/reselect

Hands On: Todo with Advanced Redux

Now in the Todo application, you can refactor everything to use the advanced techniques you have learned in the previous chapters: a middleware, an immutable data structure using JavaScript spread operators, a normalized data structure and selectors. Let's continue with the Todo application that you have build when you connected React and Redux. The last version can be found in this GitHub repository[73].

In the first part, let's use the redux-logger[74] middleware. Therefore, you have to install it on the command line:

Command Line: /

```
npm install --save redux-logger
```

Next you can use it when you create your store:

src/index.js

```
import React from 'react';
import ReactDOM from 'react-dom';
import { applyMiddleware, combineReducers, createStore } from 'redux';
import { Provider, connect } from 'react-redux';
import { createLogger } from 'redux-logger';
import './index.css';


...


// store

const rootReducer = combineReducers({
  todoState: todoReducer,
  filterState: filterReducer,
});

const logger = createLogger();

const store = createStore(
  rootReducer,
  undefined,
  applyMiddleware(logger)
);
```

---

[73]https://github.com/rwieruch/taming-the-state-todo-app/tree/3.0.0

[74]https://github.com/evgenyrodionov/redux-logger

When you start your Todo application now, you should see the output of the `logger` in the developer console of your browser when dispatching actions. The Todo application with the middleware using redux-logger can be found in this GitHub repository[75].

The second part of this chapter is using the JavaScript spread operators instead of the `Object.assign()` function to keep an immutable data structure. You can apply it in your reducer functions:

src/index.js

```
function applyAddTodo(state, action) {
  const todo = { ...action.todo, completed: false };
  return [ ...state, todo ];
}

function applyToggleTodo(state, action) {
  return state.map(todo =>
    todo.id === action.todo.id
      ? { ...todo, completed: !todo.completed }
      : todo
  );
}
```

The application should work the same as before, but this time with the spread operator for keeping an immutable data structure and thus an immutable state object. The source code can be found again in this GitHub repository[76].

In the third part of applying the advanced techniques from the previous chapters, you will use a normalized state structure. Therefore, you can install the neat library normalizr[77] on the command line:

Command Line: /

```
npm install --save normalizr
```

Let's have a look at the initial state for the `todoReducer`. You can make up an initial state for them. For instance, what about completing all coding examples in this book by having todo items for them?

---

[75]https://github.com/rwieruch/taming-the-state-todo-app/tree/4.0.0

[76]https://github.com/rwieruch/taming-the-state-todo-app/tree/5.0.0

[77]https://github.com/paularmstrong/normalizr

src/index.js

```
const todos = [
  { id: '1', name: 'Redux Standalone with advanced Actions' },
  { id: '2', name: 'Redux Standalone with advanced Reducers' },
  { id: '3', name: 'Bootstrap App with Redux' },
  { id: '4', name: 'Naive Todo with React and Redux' },
  { id: '5', name: 'Sophisticated Todo with React and Redux' },
  { id: '6', name: 'Connecting State Everywhere' },
  { id: '7', name: 'Todo with advanced Redux' },
  { id: '8', name: 'Todo but more Features' },
  { id: '9', name: 'Todo with Notifications' },
  { id: '10', name: 'Hacker News with Redux' },
];

function todoReducer(state = todos, action) {
  ...
}
```

You can use normalizr to normalize this data structure. First, you have to define a schema:

src/index.js

```
import React from 'react';
import ReactDOM from 'react-dom';
import { applyMiddleware, combineReducers, createStore } from 'redux';
import { Provider, connect } from 'react-redux';
import { createLogger } from 'redux-logger';
import { schema, normalize } from 'normalizr';
import './index.css';

// schemas

const todoSchema = new schema.Entity('todo');
```

Second, you can use the schema to normalize your initial todos and use them as default parameter in your todoReducer.

src/index.js

```
// reducers

const todos = [
  ...
];

const normalizedTodos = normalize(todos, [todoSchema]);
const initialTodoState = {
  entities: normalizedTodos.entities.todo,
  ids: normalizedTodos.result,
};

function todoReducer(state = initialTodoState, action) {
  ...
}
```

Third, your todoReducer needs to handle the normalized state structure. It has to deal with entities and a result (list of ids). You can output the normalized todos even though the Todo application crashes when you attempt to start it.

src/index.js

```
const normalizedTodos = normalize(todos, [todoSchema]);
console.log(normalizedTodos);
```

The adjusted reducer would have the following internal functions:

src/index.js

```
function applyAddTodo(state, action) {
  const todo = { ...action.todo, completed: false };
  const entities = { ...state.entities, [todo.id]: todo };
  const ids = [ ...state.ids, action.todo.id ];
  return { ...state, entities, ids };
}

function applyToggleTodo(state, action) {
  const id = action.todo.id;
  const todo = state.entities[id];
  const toggledTodo = { ...todo, completed: !todo.completed };
  const entities = { ...state.entities, [id]: toggledTodo };
```

```
return { ...state, entities };
}
```

It operates on `entities` and `ids`, because these are the output from the normalization. Last but not least, when connecting Redux with React, the components need to be aware of the normalized data structure. First, the connection between store and components:

src/index.js

```
function mapStateToPropsList(state) {
  return {
    todosAsIds: state.todoState.ids,
  };
}

function mapStateToPropsItem(state, props) {
  return {
    todo: state.todoState.entities[props.todoId],
  };
}

function mapDispatchToPropsItem(dispatch) {
  return {
    onToggleTodo: id => dispatch(doToggleTodo(id)),
  };
}

const ConnectedTodoList = connect(
  mapStateToPropsList
)(TodoList);
const ConnectedTodoItem = connect(
  mapStateToPropsItem,
  mapDispatchToPropsItem
)(TodoItem);
```

Second, the `TodoList` component receives only the `todosAsIds` and the `TodoItem` receives the `todo` entity.

src/index.js

```
function TodoApp() {
  return <ConnectedTodoList />;
}

function TodoList({ todosAsIds }) {
  return (
    <div>
      {todosAsIds.map(todoId => <ConnectedTodoItem
        key={todoId}
        todoId={todoId}
      />)}
    </div>
  );
}

function TodoItem({ todo, onToggleTodo }) {
  ...
}
```

The application should work again. Start it and play around with it. You can find the source code in the GitHub repository[78]. You have normalized your initial state structure and adjusted your reducer to deal with the new data structure.

In the fourth and last part, you are going to use selectors for your Redux architecture. This refactoring is fairly straight forward. You have to extract the parts that operate on the state in your mapStateToProps() functions to selector functions. First, define the selector functions:

src/index.js

```
// selectors

function getTodosAsIds(state) {
  return state.todoState.ids;
}

function getTodo(state, todoId) {
  return state.todoState.entities[todoId];
}
```

Second, you can use these functions instead of operating on the state directly in your mapStateTo-Props() functions:

---

[78]https://github.com/rwieruch/taming-the-state-todo-app/tree/6.0.0

src/index.js

```
// Connecting React and Redux

function mapStateToPropsList(state) {
  return {
    todosAsIds: getTodosAsIds(state),
  };
}

function mapStateToPropsItem(state, props) {
  return {
    todo: getTodo(state, props.todoId),
  };
}
```

The Todo application should work with selectors now. You can find it in the GitHub repository[79]
again.

---

[79]https://github.com/rwieruch/taming-the-state-todo-app/tree/7.0.0

Hands On: Todo but more Features

In the Todo application, there are two pieces missing feature-wise: the ability to add a todo and to filter todos by their complete state. Let's begin with the creation of a todo item. First, there needs to be a component where you can type in a todo name and execute its creation.

src/index.js

```
class TodoCreate extends React.Component {
  constructor(props) {
    super(props);

    this.state = {
      value: '',
    };

    this.onCreateTodo = this.onCreateTodo.bind(this);
    this.onChangeName = this.onChangeName.bind(this);
  }

  onChangeName(event) {
    this.setState({ value: event.target.value });
  }

  onCreateTodo(event) {
    this.props.onAddTodo(this.state.value);
    this.setState({ value: '' });
    event.preventDefault();
  }

  render() {
    return (
      <div>
        <form onSubmit={this.onCreateTodo}>
          <input
            type="text"
            placeholder="Add Todo..."
            value={this.state.value}
            onChange={this.onChangeName}
          />
          <button type="submit">Add</button>
        </form>
      </div>
```

```
    );
  }
}
```

Notice again that the component is completely unaware of Redux. It only updates its local `value` state and once the form gets submitted, it uses the local `value` state for the `onAddTodo()` callback function that's accessible in the `props` object. The component doesn't know whether the callback function updates the local state of a parent component or the Redux store. Next, you can use the connected version of this component in the `TodoApp` component.

src/index.js

```
function TodoApp() {
  return (
    <div>
      <ConnectedTodoCreate />
      <ConnectedTodoList />
    </div>
  );
}
```

The last step is to wire the React component to the Redux store by making it a connected component in the first place.

src/index.js

```
function mapDispatchToPropsCreate(dispatch) {
  return {
    onAddTodo: name => dispatch(doAddTodo(uuid(), name)),
  };
}

const ConnectedTodoCreate = connect(null, mapDispatchToPropsCreate)(TodoCreate);
```

It uses the `mapDispatchToPropsCreate()` function to get access to the dispatch method of the Redux store. The `doAddTodo()` action creator takes the name of the todo item, coming from the `TodoCreate` component, and generates a unique identifier with the `uuid()` function. The `uuid()` function is a neat little helper function that comes from the uuid[80] library. First, you have to install it:

---

[80]https://github.com/kelektiv/node-uuid

Command Line: /

```
npm install --save uuid
```

And second, you can import it to generate unique identifiers for you:

src/index.js

```
import React from 'react';
import ReactDOM from 'react-dom';
import { applyMiddleware, combineReducers, createStore } from 'redux';
import { Provider, connect } from 'react-redux';
import { createLogger } from 'redux-logger';
import { schema, normalize } from 'normalizr';
import uuid from 'uuid/v4';
import './index.css';
```

You can try to create a todo item in your Todo application now. It should work. Next you want to make use of your filter functionality to filter the list of todo items by their completed property. First, you have to add a Filter component.

src/index.js

```
function Filter({ onSetFilter }) {
  return (
    <div>
      Show
      <button
        type="button"
        onClick={() => onSetFilter('SHOW_ALL')}>
        All</button>
      <button
        type="button"
        onClick={() => onSetFilter('SHOW_COMPLETED')}>
        Completed</button>
      <button
        type="button"
        onClick={() => onSetFilter('SHOW_INCOMPLETED')}>
        Incompleted</button>
    </div>
  );
}
```

The Filter component only receives a callback function. Again it doesn't know anything about the state management that is happening above in Redux or somewhere else. The callback function is only used in different buttons to set specific filter types. You can use the connected component in the TodoApp component again.

src/index.js

```
function TodoApp() {
  return (
    <div>
      <ConnectedFilter />
      <ConnectedTodoCreate />
      <ConnectedTodoList />
    </div>
  );
}
```

Last but not least, you have to connect the Filter component to actually use it in the TodoApp component. It dispatched the doSetFilter action creator by passing the filter type from the underlying buttons in the Filter component.

src/index.js

```
function mapDispatchToPropsFilter(dispatch) {
  return {
    onSetFilter: filterType => dispatch(doSetFilter(filterType)),
  };
}

const ConnectedFilter = connect(null, mapDispatchToPropsFilter)(Filter);
```

When you start your Todo application now, you will see that the filterState will change once you click on one of your filter buttons. But nothing happens to your displayed todos. They are not filtered and that's because in your selector you select the whole list of todos. The next step would be to adjust the selector to only select the todos in the list that are matching the filter. First, you can define filter functions that match todos according to their completed state.

src/index.js

```
// filters

const VISIBILITY_FILTERS = {
  SHOW_COMPLETED: item => item.completed,
  SHOW_INCOMPLETED: item => !item.completed,
  SHOW_ALL: item => true,
};
```

Second, can use your selector to only select the todos matching a filter. You already have all selectors in place. But you need to adjust one of them to filter the todos according to the `filterState` from the Redux store.

src/index.js

```
// selectors

function getTodosAsIds(state) {
  return state.todoState.ids
    .map(id => state.todoState.entities[id])
    .filter(VISIBILITY_FILTERS[state.filterState])
    .map(todo => todo.id);
}

function getTodo(state, todoId) {
  return state.todoState.entities[todoId];
}
```

Since your state is normalized, you have to map through all your `ids` to get a list of `todos`, filter them by `filterState`, and map them back to 'ids'. That's a tradeoff you are going when normalizing your data structure, because you always have to denormalize it at some point. Your filter functionality should work once you start your application again.

You can find the final application in this GitHub repository[81]. It applies all the learnings about the Redux middleware, immutable and normalized data structures and selectors.

---

[81]https://github.com/rwieruch/taming-the-state-todo-app/tree/8.0.0

Asynchronous Redux

In the book, you have only used synchronous actions so far. There is no delay of the action dispatching involved. Yet, sometimes you want to delay an action. The example can be a simple one: Imagine you want to have a notification for your application user when a todo item was created. The notification needs to show up, but also should hide after one second. The first action would show the notification, because it sets a isShowingNotification property to true in the Redux store. Afterward, you would want to have a delayed second action to hide the notification again. In the simplest case, it would look like the following:

Code Playground

```
store.dispatch({ type: 'NOTIFICATION_SHOW', text: 'Todo created.' });
setTimeout(() => {
  store.dispatch({ type: 'NOTIFICATION_HIDE' })
}, 1000);
```

There is nothing against a simple setTimeout() function in your application. Sometimes it is easier to remember the basics in JavaScript than trying to apply yet another library to fix a problem. Since you know about actions creators, the next step could be to extract these actions into according action creators and action types.

Code Playground

```
const NOTIFICATION_SHOW = 'NOTIFICATION_SHOW';
const NOTIFICATION_HIDE = 'NOTIFICATION_HIDE';

function doShowNotification(text) {
  return {
    type: NOTIFICATION_SHOW,
    text,
  };
}

function doHideNotification() {
  return {
    type: NOTIFICATION_HIDE,
  };
}
```

```
store.dispatch(doShowNotification('Todo created.'));
setTimeout(() => {
  store.dispatch(doHideNotification());
}, 1000);
```

There are two problems in a growing application now. First, you would have to duplicate the logic of the delayed action with the setTimeout() every time you want to show a notification and hide it again. What could be helpful in this case? Right, extracting the functionality as a function. Second, once your application dispatches multiple notifications at various places at the same time, the first running action that hides a notification would hide all of them. What could be helpful in this case? Correct, you need to give each notification an identifier.

Code Playground

```
// actions
const NOTIFICATION_SHOW = 'NOTIFICATION_SHOW';
const NOTIFICATION_HIDE = 'NOTIFICATION_HIDE';

function doShowNotification(text, id) {
  return {
    type: NOTIFICATION_SHOW,
    text,
    id,
  };
}

function doHideNotification(id) {
  return {
    type: NOTIFICATION_HIDE,
    id,
  };
}

// extracted functionality
let naiveId = 0;
function showNotificationWithDelay(dispatch, text) {
  dispatch(doShowNotification(text, naiveId));
  setTimeout(() => {
    dispatch(doHideNotification(naiveId));
  }, 1000);

  naiveId++;
}
```

```
// usage
showNotificationWithDelay(store.dispatch, 'Todo created.');
```

Now each notification can be identified in the reducer and thus be either shown or hidden. The extracted function gets control over the dispatch() method from the Redux store, because it needs to dispatch a delayed action after all.

Why not passing the Redux store instead? Usually, you want to avoid to directly pass the store around. You have encountered the same reasoning in the book when weaving the Redux store for the first time into your React application. You want to make the functionalities of the store available, but not the entire store itself. That's why you only have the dispatch() method and not the entire store in your mapDispatchToProps() function when using react-redux. A connected component does never have access to the store itself and thus no other functionalities should have direct access to it to keep up with those constraints.

The pattern from above suffices for simple Redux applications that need a delayed (asynchronous) action. However, in scaling applications it has a drawback. The approach creates a second type of action. While there are synchronous actions that can be dispatched directly, as you have used them before, there are pseudo asynchronous actions, too. These pseudo asynchronous actions cannot be dispatched directly, but are used within a function that accepts the dispatch method as argument to dispatch actions eventually. That's what you have implemented with the showNotificationWithDelay() function now. Wouldn't it be great to use both types of actions the same way without worrying to pass around the dispatch method and without worrying about asynchronous or synchronous actions? You will find out about it in the next chapter.

Redux Thunk

The previous question led Dan Abramov, the creator of Redux, thinking about a general pattern to the problem of asynchronous actions. He came up with the library called redux-thunk[82] to legitimize the concept: Synchronous and asynchronous actions should be dispatched in a similar way from a Redux store. The redux-thunk library is used as middleware in your Redux store.

Code Playground

```
import { createStore, applyMiddleware } from 'redux';
import thunk from 'redux-thunk';

...

const store = createStore(
  rootReducer,
  undefined,
  applyMiddleware(thunk)
);
```

Basically, it creates a middleware for your actions creators. In this middleware, you are enabled to dispatch asynchronous actions. Apart from dispatching objects, you can dispatch functions with Redux Thunk too. Before you have always dispatched objects as actions in this book. An action itself is an object and an action creator returns an action object.

Code Playground

```
// with plain action
store.dispatch({ type: 'NOTIFICATION_SHOW', text: 'Todo created.' });

// with action creator
function doShowNotification(text) {
  return {
    type: NOTIFICATION_SHOW,
    text,
  };
}

store.dispatch(doShowNotification('Todo created.'));
```

However, now you can pass the dispatch method a function, too. The function will always give you access to the dispatch method again.

---

[82]https://github.com/gaearon/redux-thunk

Code Playground

```
// with thunk function
let naiveId = 0;
store.dispatch(function (dispatch) {
  dispatch(doShowNotification('Todo created.', naiveId));
  setTimeout(() => {
    dispatch(doHideNotification(naiveId));
  }, 1000);

  naiveId++;
});
```

The dispatch method of the Redux store when using Redux Thunk will differentiate between passed objects and functions. The passed function is called a **thunk**. You can dispatch as many actions synchronously and asynchronously as you want in a thunk. When a thunk is growing and handles complex business logic at some point in your application, it is called a **fat thunk**. You can extract a thunk function as an asynchronous action creator, that is a higher-order function and returns the thunk function, and can be dispatched the same way as a synchronous action creator.

Code Playground

```
let naiveId = 0;
function showNotificationWithDelay(text) {
  return function (dispatch) {
    dispatch(doShowNotification(text, naiveId));
    setTimeout(() => {
      dispatch(doHideNotification(naiveId));
    }, 1000);

    naiveId++;
  };
}

store.dispatch(showNotificationWithDelay('Todo created.'));
```

It is similar to the solution without Redux Thunk. However, this time you don't have to pass around the dispatch method and instead have access to it in the returned thunk function. Now, when using it in a React component, the component still only executes a callback function that it receives via its props. The connected component then dispatches an action, regardless of the action being synchronously or asynchronously, in the mapDispatchToProps() function.

That are the basics of Redux Thunk. There are a few more things that are good to know about:

- **getState():** A thunk function gives you the `getState()` method of the Redux store as second argument: `function (dispatch, getState)`. However, you should generally avoid it. It's best practice to pass all necessary state to the action creator instead of retrieving it in the thunk.
- **Promises:** Thunks work great in combination with promises. You can return a promise from your thunk and use it, for instance, to wait for its completion: `store.dispatch(showNotificationWith created.')).then(...)`.
- **Recursive Thunks:** The dispatch method in a thunk can again be used to dispatch an asynchronous action. Thus, you can apply the thunk pattern recursively.

Hands On: Todo with Notifications

After learning about asynchronous actions, the Todo application could make use of notifications, couldn't it? You can continue with the Todo application that you have built in the last chapters. As an alternative, you can clone it from this GitHub repository[83].

The first part of this hands on chapter is a great repetition on using everything you have learned before asynchronous actions. First, you have to implement a notification reducer which evaluates all actions that should generate a notification. In this case, the action that creates a todo item should be reused for the notification. That's the great thing about Redux: All reducers who care about an action can make use of it. Also the id of the todo item can be used to store the notification with its own identifier to hide it later again.

src/index.js

```
function notificationReducer(state = {}, action) {
  switch(action.type) {
    case TODO_ADD : {
      return applySetNotifyAboutAddTodo(state, action);
    }
    default : return state;
  }
}

function applySetNotifyAboutAddTodo(state, action) {
  const { name, id } = action.todo;
  return { ...state, [id]: 'Todo Created: ' + name  };
}
```

Second, you have to include the reducer in your combined reducer to make it accessible to the Redux store.

---

src/index.js

```
const rootReducer = combineReducers({
  todoState: todoReducer,
  filterState: filterReducer,
  notificationState: notificationReducer,
});
```

The Redux part is done. It is only a reducer that you need to include in the Redux store. The action gets reused. Third, you have to implement a React component that displays all of your notifications.

src/index.js

```
function Notifications({ notifications }) {
  return (
    <div>
      {notifications.map(note => <div key={note}>{note}</div>)}
    </div>
  );
}
```

Fourth, you can include the connected version of the Notifications component in your TodoApp component.

src/index.js

```
function TodoApp() {
  return (
    <div>
      <ConnectedFilter />
      <ConnectedTodoCreate />
      <ConnectedTodoList />
      <ConnectedNotifications />
    </div>
  );
}
```

Last but not least, you have to wire up React and Redux in the connected ConnectedNotifications component.

src/index.js

```
function mapStateToPropsNotifications(state, props) {
  return {
    notifications: getNotifications(state),
  };
}

const ConnectedNotifications = connect(mapStateToPropsNotifications)(Notificatio\
ns);
```

The only thing left is to implement the missing selector getNotifications(). Since the notifications in the Redux store are saved as an object, because they are a map of identifier and notification pairs, you have to use a helper function to convert it into an array. You can extract the helper function, because you might need such functionalities more often and shouldn't couple it to the domain of notifications.

src/index.js

```
function getNotifications(state) {
  return getArrayOfObject(state.notificationState);
}

function getArrayOfObject(object) {
  return Object.keys(object).map(key => object[key]);
}
```

The first part of this chapter is done. You should see a notification in your Todo application once you create a todo item. The second part will implement a NOTIFICATION_HIDE action and use it in the notificationReducer to remove the notification from the state again. First, you have to introduce the action type:

src/index.js

```
const TODO_ADD = 'TODO_ADD';
const TODO_TOGGLE = 'TODO_TOGGLE';
const FILTER_SET = 'FILTER_SET';
const NOTIFICATION_HIDE = 'NOTIFICATION_HIDE';
```

Second, you can implement an action creator that uses the action type. It will hide (remove) the notification by id, because they are stored by id in the Redux store:

src/index.js

```
function doHideNotification(id) {
  return {
    type: NOTIFICATION_HIDE,
    id
  };
}
```

Third, you can capture it in the new notificationReducer. The JavaScript destructuring functionality can be used to omit a property from an object. You can simply omit the notification and return the remaining object. It is a neat trick if you want to get rid of a property in an object when knowing its key.

src/index.js

```
function notificationReducer(state = {}, action) {
  switch(action.type) {
    case TODO_ADD : {
      return applySetNotifyAboutAddTodo(state, action);
    }
    case NOTIFICATION_HIDE : {
      return applyRemoveNotification(state, action);
    }
    default : return state;
  }
}

function applyRemoveNotification(state, action) {
  const {
    [action.id]: notificationToRemove,
    ...restNotifications,
  } = state;
  return restNotifications;
}
```

That was the second part of this chapter that introduced the hiding notification functionality. But you don't make any use of the functionality yet. The third and last part of this chapter will introduce asynchronous actions to hide a notification after a couple of seconds. As mentioned earlier, you wouldn't need a library to solve this problem. You could simply built up on the JavaScript setTimeout() functionality. But for the sake of learning about asynchronous actions in Redux, you will use Redux Thunk. It's up to you to exchange it with another asynchronous actions library afterward for the sake of learning about the alternatives. You will hear about these alternative libraries later.

First, you have to install the redux-thunk[84] library on the command line:

Command Line: /

```
npm install --save redux-thunk
```

Second, you can import it in your code:

src/index.js

```
...

import thunk from 'redux-thunk';

...
```

And third, use it in your Redux store middleware:

src/index.js

```
const store = createStore(
  rootReducer,
  undefined,
  applyMiddleware(thunk, logger)
);
```

The application should still work. When using Redux Thunk, you can dispatch action objects as you did before. However, now you can dispatch thunks (functions), too. Rather than dispatching an action object that only creates a todo item, you can dispatch a thunk function that creates a todo item and hides the notification about the creation after a couple of seconds. You have two plain actions creators, doAddTodo() and doHideNotification(), already in place. You only have to use them in your thunk function.

---

[84]https://github.com/gaearon/redux-thunk

src/index.js

```
function doAddTodoWithNotification(id, name) {
  return function (dispatch) {
    dispatch(doAddTodo(id, name));

    setTimeout(function () {
      dispatch(doHideNotification(id));
    }, 5000);
  }
}
```

In the last step, you have to use the doAddTodoWithNotification() rather than the doAddTodo() action creator when connecting Redux and React in your TodoCreate component.

src/index.js

```
function mapDispatchToPropsCreate(dispatch) {
  return {
    onAddTodo: name => dispatch(
      doAddTodoWithNotification(uuid(), name)
    ),
  };
}
```

That's it. Your notifications should work and hide after five seconds now. Basically, you have built the foundation for a notification system in your Todo application. You can use it for other actions, too. For instance, when completing a todo item you could trigger a notification too. The project can be found again in this GitHub repository[85].

---

[85]https://github.com/rwieruch/taming-the-state-todo-app/tree/9.0.0

Asynchronous Actions Alternatives

The whole concept around asynchronous actions led to a handful of libraries which solve this particular issue. Redux Thunk was only the first one introduced by Dan Abramov. However, he agrees that there are use cases where Redux Thunk doesn't solve the problem in an efficient way. Redux Thunk can be used when you encounter a use case for asynchronous actions for the first time. But when there are more complex scenarios involved, you can use advanced solutions beyond Redux Thunk.

All of these solutions address the problem as side-effects in Redux. Asynchronous actions are used to deal with those side-effects. They are most often used when performing impure operations which happen to be often asynchronous too: fetching data from an API, delaying an execution (e.g. hiding a notification), or accessing the browser cache. All these operations are asynchronous and impure, hence are solved with asynchronous actions. In an application, that uses the functional programming paradigm, you want to have all these impure operations on the edge of your application. You don't want to have these close to your core application.

This chapter briefly shows the alternatives that you can use instead of Redux Thunk. Among all the different alternatives, I only want to introduce you to the most popular and innovative ones.

Redux Saga

Redux Saga[86] is the most popular asynchronous actions library for Redux. *"The mental model is that a saga is like a separate thread in your application that's solely responsible for side effects."* Basically, it outsources the impure operations into separate threads. These threads can be started, paused or cancelled with plain Redux actions from your core application. Thereby, threads in Redux Saga make it simple to keep your side-effects away from your core application. However, threads can dispatch actions and have access to the state though.

Redux Saga uses JavaScript ES6 Generators[87] as underlying technology. That's why the code reads like synchronous code. You avoid it having callback functions. The advantage over Redux Thunk is that your actions stay pure and thus they can be tested well.

Apart from Redux Thunk and Redux Sage, there are other side-effect libraries for Redux. If you want to try out observables in JavaScript, you could give Redux Observable[88] a shot. It builds up on RxJS, a generic library for reactive programming. If you are interested in another library that uses reactive programming principles, too, you can try Redux Cycles[89].

In conclusion, as you can see, all these libraries, Redux Saga, Redux Observable and Redux Cycles, make use of different techniques in JavaScript. You can give them a try to experiment with recent JavaScript technologies: generators or observables. The whole ecosystem around asynchronous actions is a great playground to try new things in JavaScript in the end.

---

[86]https://github.com/redux-saga/redux-saga

[87]https://developer.mozilla.org/en/docs/Web/JavaScript/Reference/Global_Objects/Generator

[88]https://github.com/redux-observable/redux-observable

[89]https://github.com/cyclejs-community/redux-cycles

Hands On: Todo with Redux Saga

In a previous chapter, you used Redux Thunk to dispatch asynchronous actions. These were used to add a todo item with a notification whereas the notification vanishes after a couple of seconds again. In this chapter you will use Redux Saga instead of Redux Thunk. Therefore, you can install the former library and uninstall the latter one. You can continue with your previous Todo application.

Command Line: /

```
npm uninstall --save redux-thunk
npm install --save redux-saga
```

The action you have used before with a thunk becomes a pure action creator now. It will be used to start the saga thread.

src/index.js

```
const TODO_ADD_WITH_NOTIFICATION = 'TODO_ADD_WITH_NOTIFICATION';

...

function doAddTodoWithNotification(id, name) {
  return {
    type: TODO_ADD_WITH_NOTIFICATION,
    todo: { id, name },
  };
}
```

Now you can introduce your first saga that listens on this particular action, because the action is solely used to start the saga thread.

src/index.js

```
import { takeEvery } from 'redux-saga/effects';

...

// sagas

function* watchAddTodoWithNotification() {
  yield takeEvery(TODO_ADD_WITH_NOTIFICATION, ...);
}
```

Most often you will find one part of the saga watching incoming actions and evaluating them. If an evaluation applies truthfully, it will often call another generator function, identified with the asterisk, that handles the side-effect. That way, you can keep your side-effect watcher maintainable and don't clutter them with business logic. In the previous example, a takeEvery() effect of Redux Saga is used to handle every action with the specified action type. Yet there are other effects in Redux Saga such as takeLatest() which only takes the last of the incoming actions by action type.

src/index.js

```
import { delay } from 'redux-saga';
import { put, takeEvery } from 'redux-saga/effects';

function* watchAddTodoWithNotification() {
  yield takeEvery(TODO_ADD_WITH_NOTIFICATION, handleAddTodoWithNotification);
}

function* handleAddTodoWithNotification(action) {
  const { todo } = action;
  const { id, name } = todo;
  yield put(doAddTodo(id, name));
  yield delay(5000);
  yield put(doHideNotification(id));
}
```

As you can see, in JavaScript generators you use the yield statement to execute asynchronous code synchronously. Only when the function after the yield resolves, the code will execute the next line of code. Redux Saga comes with helper functions such as delay() that can be used to delay the execution by an amount of time. It would be the same as using setTimeout() in JavaScript, but the delay() helper makes it more concise when using JavaScript generators and can be used in a synchronous way when using the yield statement.

In the end, you only have to exchange your middleware in your Redux store from using Redux Thunk to Redux Saga.

src/index.js

```
import createSagaMiddleware, { delay } from 'redux-saga';
import { put, takeEvery } from 'redux-saga/effects';

...

const rootReducer = combineReducers({
  todoState: todoReducer,
  filterState: filterReducer,
```

```
  notificationState: notificationReducer,
});

const logger = createLogger();
const saga = createSagaMiddleware();

const store = createStore(
  rootReducer,
  undefined,
  applyMiddleware(saga, logger)
);

saga.run(watchAddTodoWithNotification);
```

That's it. You Todo application should run with Redux Saga instead of Redux Thunk now. The final application can be found in the GitHub repository[90] again. In the future, it is up to you to decide on an asynchronous actions library when using Redux. Is it Redux Thunk or Redux Saga? Or do you decide to try something new with Redux Observable or Redux Cycles? The Redux ecosystem is full of amenities to try cutting edge JavaScript features such as generators or observables. However, you need to decide yourself if you need a asynchronous actions library in the first place.

[90]https://github.com/rwieruch/taming-the-state-todo-app/tree/10.0.0

Redux Patterns, Techniques and Best Practices

There are several patterns and best practices that you can apply in a Redux application. I will go through a handful of them to point you in the right direction. However, the evolving patterns and best practices around the ecosystem are changing all the time. You will want to read more about these topics on your own.

Using JavaScript ES6

So far, you have written your Redux code mostly in JavaScript ES5. Redux is inspired by the functional programming paradigm and uses a lot of its concepts: immutable data structures and pure functions. When using Redux in your scaling application, you will often find yourself using pure functions that solve only one problem. For instance, an action creator only returns an action object, a reducer only returns the new state and a selector only returns derived properties. You will embrace this mental model and use it in Redux agnostic code, too. You will see yourself more often using functions that only solve one problem, using higher-order functions to return functions and compose functions into each other. You will move toward a functional programming style with Redux.

JavaScript ES6 and beyond complements the functional programming style in JavaScript perfectly. You only have to look at the following example to understand how much more concisely higher-order functions can be written with JavaScript ES6 arrow functions.

Code Playground

```
// JavaScript ES5
function higherOrderFunction(foo) {
  return function (bar) {

      ...

  };
}

// JavaScript ES6
const higherOrderFunction = (foo) => (bar) => { ... };
```

It's a higher-order function that is much more readable in JavaScript ES6. You will find yourself using higher-order functions more often when programming in a functional style. It will happen that you not only use one higher-order function, but a higher-order function that returns a higher-order function that returns a function. Again it becomes easier to read when using JavaScript ES6.

Code Playground

```
// JavaScript ES5
function higherOrderFunction(foo) {
  return function (bar) {
    return function (qwe) {

      ...

    }
  };
}
```

```
// JavaScript ES6
const higherOrderFunction = (foo) => (bar) => (qwe) => { ... };
```

I encourage you to apply these in your Redux code. It would turn out the following way:

Code Playground

```
// action creator
const doAddTodo = (id, name) => ({
  type: ADD_TODO,
  todo: { id, name },
});

// selector
const getTodos = (state) => state.todos;

// action creators using Redux Thunk
const showNotificationWithDelay = (text) => (dispatch) => {
  dispatch(doShowNotification(text));
  setTimeout(() => dispatch(doHideNotification()), 1000);
}
```

The JavaScript community made a great shift toward functional programming with the rising popularity of React and Redux. Functional programming let's you write more predictable code by embracing pure functions, raising awareness about side-effects, and keeping data structures immutable. JavaScript ES6 and beyond make it easier and more readable to write in a functional style.

Naming Conventions

In Redux, you have a handful of different types of functions. You have action creators, selectors and reducers. It is always good to name them accordingly to their type. Other developers will have an easier time identifying the function type. Just following a naming convention for your functions, you can give yourself and others valuable information about the function itself.

Personally, I follow this naming convention with Redux functions. It uses prefixes for each function type:

- action creators: **do**Something
- reducers: **apply**Something
- selectors: **get**Something
- sagas: **watch**Something, **handle**Something

In the previous chapters, the example code always used this naming convention. In addition, it clarifies things when using higher-order functions. Remember the `mapDispatchToProps()` function when connecting Redux to React?

Code Playground

```
const mapStateToProps = (state) => ({
  todos: getTodos(state),
});

const mapDispatchToProps = (dispatch) => ({
  onToggleTodo: (id) => dispatch(doToggleTodo(id)),
});
```

The functions themselves become more concise by using JavaScript ES6 arrow functions. But there is another clue that makes proper naming so powerful. Solely from a naming perspective, you can see that the `mapStateToProps()` and `mapDispatchToProps()` functions transform the returned properties from the Redux world to the React world. The connected component doesn't know about selectors or actions creators anymore. As you can see, that is already expressed in the transformed props and functions. They are named `todos` and `onToggleTodo`. There are no remains from the Redux world, from a technical perspective but also from a pure naming perspective. That's powerful, because your underlying components are Redux agnostic.

So far, the chapter was only about the naming of functions in the Redux world. But there is another part in Redux that can be named properly: action types. Consider the following action type names:

Code Playground

```
const ADD_TODO = 'ADD_TODO';
const TODO_ADD = 'TODO_ADD';
```

Most cultures read from left to right. That's conveyed in programming, too. So which action type naming makes more sense? Is it the verb or the subject? You can decide on your own, but become clear about a consistent naming convention for your action types. Personally, I find it easier to scan when I have the subject, the domain in this case, first. When using Redux Logger in a scaling application where a handful actions can be dispatched at once, I find it easier to scan by subject than by verb. You can even go one step further and apply the subject as domain prefix for your action types:

Code Playground

```
const todo/ADD = 'todo/ADD';
```

These are only opinionated naming conventions for these types of functions and constants (action types) in Redux. You can come up with your own. But do yourself and your fellow developers a favor and reach an agreement first and then apply them consistently through your code base.

The Relationship between Actions and Reducers

Actions and reducers are not strictly coupled. They only share an action type. A dispatched action, for example with the action type TODO_ADD, can be captured in multiple reducers that utilize TODO_-ADD. You have done it before in the todoReducer and notificationReducer. That's an important fact when implementing a larger state management architecture in your application.

When coming from an object-oriented programming background though, you might abuse actions/reducers as setters and selectors as getters. You will couple actions and reducers in a 1:1 relationship. I will call it the **command pattern** in Redux. It can be useful in some scenarios, as I will point out later, but in general it's not the philosophy of Redux.

Redux can be seen as event bus of your application. You can send events (actions) with a payload and an identifier (action type) into the bus and it will pass potential consumer (reducers). Only a part of these consumers is interested in the event. That's what I call the **event pattern** that Redux embraces.

You can say that the higher you place your actions on the spectrum of abstraction, the more reducers are interested in it. The action becomes an event. The lower you place your actions on the spectrum of abstraction, the less reducers are interested in it. In the end, most often only one reducer can consume it when it is placed on a lower place of the spectrum of abstraction. The action becomes a command. It is a concrete action rather than an abstract action. It is important to note, though, that you have to keep the balance between abstraction and concreteness. Too abstract actions can lead to a mess when too many reducers consume it. Too concrete actions might only be used by one reducer all the time. Most developers run into the latter scenario though. In Redux, obviously depending on your application, it should be a healthy balance of both.

In the book, you have encountered a relationship of 1:1 between action and reducer most of the time (except for the TODO_ADD action). Let's take an action that completes a todo item as demonstration:

Code Playground

```
function doCompleteTodo(id) {
  return {
    type: TODO_COMPLETE,
    todo: { id },
  };
}

function todosReducer(state = [], action) {
  switch(action.type) {
    case TODO_COMPLETE : {
      return applyCompleteTodo(state, action);
    }
    default : return state;
```

```
    }
}
```

Now, imagine that there should be a measuring of the progress of the Todo application user. The progress will always start at zero when the user opens the application. When a todo gets completed, the progress should increase by one. A potentially easy solution could be counting all completed todo items. However, since there could be completed todo items already, and you want to measure the completed todo items in this session, the solution would not suffice. The solution could be a second reducer that counts the completed todos in this session.

Code Playground

```
function progressReducer(state = 0, action) {
  switch(action.type) {
    case TODO_COMPLETE : {
      return state++;
    }
    default : return state;
  }
}
```

The counter will increment when a todo got completed. Now, you can easily measure the progress of your users when they complete todo items. Suddenly, you have a 1:2 relationship between action and reducer. The action that is used for completing a todo item is consumed by two reducers. Nobody forces you not to couple action and reducer in a 1:1 relationship, but it always makes sense to be creative in this manner. What would happen otherwise? Regarding the progress measurement issue, you might have to come up with a second action type and couple it to the previous reducer:

Code Playground

```
function doTrackProgress() {
  return {
    type: PROGRESS_TRACK,
  };
}

function progressReducer(state = 0, action) {
  switch(action.type) {
    case PROGRESS_TRACK : {
      roturn state++;
    }
    default : return state;
  }
}
```

The action would be dispatched in parallel with the COMPLETE TODO action.

Code Playground

```
dispatch(doCompleteTodo('0'));
dispatch(doTrackProgress());
```

But that would miss the point in Redux. You would want to come up with these commonalities to make your actions more abstract and be used by multiple reducers. My rule of thumb for this: Approach your actions as concrete actions with a 1:1 relationship to their reducers, but keep yourself always open to reuse them as more abstract actions in other reducers.

Folder Organization

Eventually, your Redux application grows and you cannot manage everything - reducers, action creators, selectors, store and view - in one file. You will have to split up the files. Fortunately, JavaScript ES6 brings import[91] and export[92] statements to distribute functionalities in files. If you are not familiar with these, you should read about them.

In this chapter, I want to show you two approaches to organize your folder and files in a Redux application. The first approach, the **technical folder organization**, is used in smaller applications. Once your application scales and more than one team in your organization is working on the project, you can consider the **feature folder organization**. In addition, you will learn about best practices for your file and folder structure in this chapter.

Technical Folder Organization

The technical separation of concerns is used in smaller applications. Basically, in my opinion, there are two requirements to use this approach:

- the application is managed by only one person or one team, thus has less conflict potential when working on the same code base
- the application is small from a lines of code perspective and *can* be managed by one person or one team

In conclusion, it depends on the size of the team and the size of the code base. Now, how to separate the files? They get separated by their technical aspects:

Folder Organization

```
-app
--reducers
--actions creators
--selectors
--store
--constants
--components
```

The reducers, action creators, selectors and store should be clear. In these folders you have all the different aspects of Redux. In the components folder you have your view layer. When using React, that would be the place where you will find your React components. In the constants folder you can have any constants, but also the action types of Redux. These can be imported in the action creators and reducers. An elaborated folder/file organization split by technical aspects might look like the following:

---

[91]https://developer.mozilla.org/en/docs/Web/JavaScript/Reference/Statements/import
[92]https://developer.mozilla.org/en/docs/Web/JavaScript/Reference/Statements/export

Folder Organization

```
-app
--reducers
---todoReducer.js
---filterReducer.js
---notificationReducer.js
--actions creators
---filters.js
---todos.js
---notifications.js
--selectors
---filters.js
---todos.js
---notifications.js
--store
---store.js
--constants
---actionTypes.js
--components
---TodoList.js
---TodoItem.js
---Filter.js
---Notifications.js
```

What are the advantages and disadvantages of this approach? The most important advantage is that reducers and action creators are not coupled. They are loosely arranged in their folders. It embraces the notion of Redux to capture any action in any reducer. Reducers and action creators are not in a 1:1 relationship. In addition, all Redux functionalities are reachable from a top level. None of these functionalities are hidden in a lower level and thus less accessible. This approach embraces the event pattern which was mentioned before. A disadvantage of this approach, hence the two requirements, is that it doesn't scale well. Each technical folder will grow endlessly. There are no constraints except for the separation by type. It can become messy after you have introduced several reducers, action creators and selectors.

Feature Folder Organization

The second approach, the separation by feature, is most often used in larger applications. You have a greater flexibility in grouping the features, because you can always split up bigger features to smaller ones and thus keep the folders lightweight.

Folder Organization

```
-app
--todo
--filter
--notification
--store
```

An elaborated folder/file organization might look like the following:

Folder Organization

```
-app
--todo
---TodoList.js
---TodoItem.js
---reducer.js
---actionCreators.js
---selectors.js
--filter
---Filter.js
---reducer.js
---actionCreators.js
---selectors.js
--notification
---Notifications.js
---reducer.js
---actionCreators.js
---selectors.js
--store
---store.js
```

This approach, separating by features, is way more flexible than the previous approach. It gives you more freedom to arrange your folders and files as features. When using this approach, there are more ways to accomplish it. You don't necessarily have to follow the example above.

What are the advantages and disadvantages of this approach? It has the same advantages and disadvantages as the technical folder organization but negated. Instead of making action creators and reducers accessible on a top level, they are hidden in a feature folder. In a scaling application with multiple teams, other teams will most likely not reuse your action creators and reducers but implement their own. Another disadvantage is that it groups action creators and reducers in a 1:1 relationship which goes against the overarching idea of Redux. You embrace a command pattern instead of an event pattern. The advantage on the other side, and that's why most teams in a scaling application are using this approach, is that it grows well. Teams can work on separate feature folders and don't run into conflicts. Still, they can follow the overarching state management flow, when using a middleware library like redux-logger.

Even though the feature folder organization bears a lot of pitfalls by embracing the command pattern which was mentioned earlier, it is often used in scaling applications with several development teams. Therefore, I can give one crucial advice to this approach: Try to make your action creators, reducers and selectors accessible to everyone so that they can be reused. It can happen by documentation, word of mouth or another variation of folder/file organization.

Ducks

In Redux, there exists another concept called ducks. It relates to the organization of action creators, action types and reducers as tuples. The ducks concept bundles these tuples into self contained modules. Often, these modules end up being only one file. The official ducks pattern has a bunch of guidelines which you can read up in the GitHub repository[93]. However, you wouldn't need to apply all of these. For instance, in the Todo application a duck file for the filter domain might look like the following:

Code Playground

```
const FILTER_SET = 'FILTER_SET';

function filterReducer(state = 'SHOW_ALL', action) {
  switch(action.type) {
    case FILTER_SET : {
      return applySetFilter(state, action);
    }
    default : return state;
  }
}

function applySetFilter(state, action) {
  return action.filter;
}

function doSetFilter(filter) {
  return {
    type: FILTER_SET,
    filter,
  };
}
```

---

[93]https://github.com/erikras/ducks-modular-redux

```
export default filterReducer;

export {
  doSetFilter,
};
```

The same file structure would apply for the notification feature and the todo feature itself. The drawbacks of the ducks concept are similar to the feature folder approach. You couple actions and reducers, hence no one will embrace to capture actions in multiple reducers. As long as action and reducer are coupled, the ducks concept makes sense. Otherwise, it shouldn't be applied too often. Instead, you should embrace the idea of Redux to keep your reducers and action creators accessible on a top level.

Testing

The book will not dive deeply into the topic of testing, but it shouldn't be unmentioned. Testing your code in programming is essential and should be seen as mandatory. You want to keep the quality of your code high and an assurance that everything works. However, testing your code can often be tedious. You have to setup, mock or spy things before you can finally start to test it. Or you you have to cover a ton of edge cases in your one huge code block. But I can give you comfort by saying that this is not the case when testing state management done with Redux. I will show you how you can easily test the necessary parts, keep your efforts low and stay lazy.

Perhaps you have heard about the testing pyramid. There are end-to-end tests, integration tests and unit tests. If you are not familiar with those, the book gives you a quick and basic overview. A unit test is used to test an isolated and small block of code. It can be a single function that is tested by an unit test. However, sometimes the units work well in isolation yet don't work in combination with other units. They need to be tested as a group as units. That's where integration tests can help out by covering whether units work well together. Last but not least, an end-to-end test is the simulation of a real user scenario. It could be an automated setup in a browser simulating the login flow of an user in a web application. While unit tests are fast and easy to write and to maintain, end-to-end tests are the opposite of this spectrum.

How many tests do I need of each type? You want to have many unit tests to cover your isolated functions. After that, you can have several integration tests to cover that the most important functions work in combination as expected. Last but not least, you might want to have only a few end-to-end tests to simulate critical scenarios in your web application. That's it for the general excursion in the world of testing. Now, how does it apply to state management with Redux?

Redux embraces the functional programming style. Your functions are pure and you don't have to worry about any side-effects. A function always returns the same output for the same input. Such functions are easy to test, because you only have to give them an input and expect the output because there is a no side-effect guarantee. That's the perfect fit for unit tests, isn't it? In conclusion, it makes state management testing when build with Redux a pleasure.

In Redux, you have different groups of functions: action creators, reducers, selectors. For each of these groups, you can see a pattern for their input and output. These can be applied to a test pattern which can be used as blueprint for a unit test for each group of functions.

Input Pattern:

- action creators can have an optional input that becomes their optional payload
- selectors can have an optional input that supports them to select the substate
- reducers will always receive a previous state and action

Output Pattern:

- action creators will always return an object with a type and optional payload

- selectors will always return a substate of the state
- reducers will always return a new state

Test Pattern:

- when invoking an action creator, the correct return object should be expected
- when invoking a selector, the correct substate should be expected
- when invoking a reducer, the correct new state should be expected

How does that apply in code? The book will show it in pseudo code, because it will not make any assumption about your testing libraries. Yet it should be sufficient to pick up these patterns for each group of functions (action creators, reducers, selectors) to apply them in your unit tests.

Action Creators:

Code Playground

```
// whereas the payload is optional
const payload = { ... };

const action = doSomething(payload);
const expectedAction = {
  type: 'DO_SOMETHING',
  payload,
};

expect(action).to.equal(expectedAction);
```

Selectors:

Code Playground

```
// whereas the payload is optional
const state = { ... };
const payload = { ... };

const substate = getSomething(state, payload);
const expectedSubstate = { ... };

expect(substate).to.equal(expectedSubstate)
```

Reducers:

Code Playground

```
const previousState = { ... };
const action = {
  type: 'DO_SOMETHING',
  payload,
};

const newState = someReducer(previousState, action);
const expectedNewState = { ... };

expect(newState).to.equal(expectedNewState);
```

These test patterns will always stay the same for their aspects in Redux. You only have to fill in the blanks. You can even give yourself an easier time and setup automated code snippets for your editor of choice. For instance, typing "rts" (abbr. for "redux test selector") gives you the blueprint for a selector test. The other two snippets could be "rtr" (redux test reducer) and "rta" (redux test action). After that, you only have to fill in the remaining things.

These test patterns for state management show you how simple testing becomes when working with the clear constraints of a library like Redux. Everything behaves the same, it is predictable, and thus can be tested every time the in the same way. When setting up automated code snippets, you will save yourself a lot of time, yet have a great test coverage for your whole state management. You can even go one step further and apply test-driven development (TDD)[94] which basically means you test before you implement.

There is another neat helper that can ensure that your state stays immutable. Because you never know if you accidentally mutate your state even though it is forbidden in Redux. I guess, there is a handful of libraries around this topic, but I use deep-freeze[95] in my tests to ensure that the state (and even actions) doesn't get mutated.

Code Playground

```
import deepFreeze from 'deep-freeze';

const previousState = { ... };
const action = {
  type: 'DO_SOMETHING',
  payload,
};

deepFreeze(previousState);
```

---

[94]https://en.wikipedia.org/wiki/Test-driven_development
[95]https://github.com/substack/deep-freeze

```
const newState = someReducer(previousState, action);
const expectedNewState = { ... };

expect(newState).to.equal(expectedNewState);
```

That's it for testing your different aspects when using Redux. It can be accomplished by using unit tests. You could apply integration tests, too, for instance to test an action creator and reducer altogether. After all, you have a blueprint for testing these functions all the time at your hand and there is no excuse anymore to not test your code. If you want to dive into a testing setup for your React application, checkout this React testing setup and usage walkthrough[96].

---

[96]https://www.robinwieruch.de/react-testing-tutorial/

Error Handling

The topic of error handling is rarely touched in programming. Often, the topic is avoided by the community and it is hard to find a common sense about it. This chapter gives you basic guidance on how you could provide error handling in your Redux application.

Error handling is often involved when making requests to an API. You have learned about asynchronous actions in Redux that can be used for these kind of side-effects. But there was no saying about error handling in those side-effects so far. How to catch the errors and how to make them visible for your application end-user?

Basically, an error in an application can be represented as a state. That's why the topic is discussed in a state management book in the first place. For instance, imagine that you get your todo items from a server request. You would have an API on the server-side that exposes these todo items. Once you fetch these todo items from the API, you would have to deal with error handling, because a request can always fail. The following request returns a JavaScript promise. The fetch can be either successfully resolved in a then() method or yields an error in a catch() method.

Code Playground

```
fetch('my/todos/api').then(function(response) {
  return response.json();
}).then(function(todos) {
  // do something with todos
}).catch(function(error) {
  // do something with error
});
```

When using Redux asynchronous actions with Redux Thunk, the request could live in a thunk:

Code Playground

```
function getTodos(dispatch) {
  fetch('my/todos/api').then(function(response) {
    return response.json();
  }).then(function(todos) {
    // do something with todos
  }).catch(function(error) {
    // do something with error
  });
}
```

Now, it would be up to you to store either the todos or the error as state in your Redux store. You could have two potential actions:

Code Playground

```
const TODOS_FETCH_SUCCESS = 'TODOS_FETCH_SUCCESS';
const TODOS_FETCH_ERROR = 'TODOS_FETCH_ERROR';
```

These could be used in your Redux Thunk to store both potential outcomes:

Code Playground

```
function getTodos(dispatch) {
  fetch('my/todos/api').then(function(response) {
    return response.json();
  }).then(function(todos) {
    dispatch({ type: TODOS_FETCH_SUCCESS, todos });
  }).catch(function(error) {
    dispatch({ type: TODOS_FETCH_ERROR, error });
  });
}
```

The todo reducer would have to deal with both actions now. One that stores the todo items and one that stores the error object.

Code Playground

```
const initialState = {
  todos: [],
  error: null,
};

function reducer(state = initialState, action) {
  switch(action.type) {
    case 'TODOS_FETCH_SUCCESS' : {
      return applyFetchTodosSuccess(state, action);
    }
    case 'TODOS_FETCH_ERROR' : {
      return applyFetchTodosError(state, action);
    }
    default : return state;
  }
}

...
```

That's it basically for the state management part. Whereas the `applyFetchTodosError()` function would set the error object in the state, the `applyFetchTodosSuccess()` function would set the list of todos. In addition, the success function would have to reset the error property in the state to null again, because imagine you would do a second request after the first request has failed. When the second request was successful, you would want to store the todo items but reset the error state.

In your view layer, depending on the todo state, you could decide whether to show an error message, because there is an error object in the todo state, or to show the list of todos. When there is an error message displayed, you could provide your end-user with a button to try fetching the todos again. When the second request is successful, the error object is set to null and instead the todo items are set in the state. The view layer could display the list of todo items now.

After all, there is no magic behind error handling in Redux. Whenever an error occurs, you would store it in your state. When the view layer notices an error in the state, it could use conditional rendering to show an error message instead of the assumed result.

(React in) Redux FAQ

I intend to grow this section organically to answer frequently asked questions to the best of my knowledge. These are questions that come up often when discussing Redux standalone or as complementing part of React.

Redux vs. Local State

When introducing Redux to a React application, people are unsure how to treat the local state with `this.state` and `this.setState()`. Should they replace the local state entirely with Redux or keep a mix of both? The larger part of the community would argue that it is the latter and I agree with it. Local state doesn't become obsolete when using a sophisticated state management library such as Redux. You would still use it.

Imagine your application grows in lines of code and in number of developers working on this application. Your global state in Redux will necessarily grow, too. However, you want to keep the global state meaningful and reusable from multiple parties (developers, components) in your application. That's why not everything should end up in the global state. In a growing application, you should always revisit your global state and make sure that it is not cluttered and arranged thoughtfully.

The cluttering happens when too much state ends up in the global state that is only used by a single party (one component, one part of the component tree). You should think twice about this kind of state and evaluate whether it would make more sense to put in the local state. Always ask yourself: Who is interested in this state? A balanced mixture of local state and sophisticated state will make your application maintainable and predictable in the long run.

The boundaries between local state and sophisticated state will blur when using a state management library like MobX as alternative to Redux. You will learn about MobX later in this book. But there too, you can plan your state thoughtfully in advance in your application.

In general, the usage of Redux state should be kept to a minimum. A good rule of thumb is to keep the state close to your component with local state but evaluate later whether another party is interested in the state. If another party manages an equivalent state structure in its local state, you could use a reusable higher-order component that manages the state. If the state is shared, you could try to lift your state up or down the component hierarchy. However, if lifting state doesn't solve the problem for you, because the state is shared across the application, you should consider to use Redux for it. In the end, after revisiting all your possibilities when only using React's local state, you might not need Redux in your application.

View vs. Entity State

In the beginning of the book, I differentiated between view state and entity state. Imagine you have a page that does both displaying a list of items and showing opt-in modals for each item to remove or edit the item. While the former would be the entity state, the latter would be the view state. The entity state, the list of items, most often comes from a backend application. But the view state is triggered by the user only in the frontend. Is there a pattern of where to store which kind of state?

The entity state often comes from the backend. It is fetched asynchronously. In applications, you want to avoid to fetch entities more than once. A good practice would be to fetch the entities once and not again when they are already there. Thus, they would have to be stored somewhere where several parties know that these entities are already fetched. The global state is a perfect place to store them.

The view state is altered only in the frontend. Often, it isn't shared across the application, because, for instance, only the modal knows if it is opened or closed. Since it doesn't need to be shared, you can use the local state and avoid to clutter in the global state.

Imagine you have a component that has tabs. Each tab gives you the possibility to change the representation of displayed items. For instance, the user can choose a grid or a list layout ti display items. It is absolutely fine to store this state in the local state. In addition, you can give your user an improved user experience. You could store the selected tab in the local storage of your browser, too, and when the user returns to the page, you rehydrate the state from the local storage into your local state. The user will always find their preferred tab as the selected one.

Accidental vs. Planned State

Can you plan your state? I would argue that you can plan it. You can plan which part of the state goes into the global state and which part goes into the local state. For instance, you know about the view and entity states. In addition, you can put some of your state in the local storage to improve the user experience. However, in an evolving application, your state grows and the structure changes. What can you do about it? My recommendation is always revisiting your state arrangements and structure. There is always room for improvements. You should refactor it early to keep it maintainable and predictable in the long run.

Redux State as Architecture

The book taught you the practical usage of Redux. You have learned about the main parts in the Redux state management architecture: actions, reducers and the store.

Concept Playground

```
Action -> Reducer(s) -> Store
```

The chain is connected to the view layer by something (e.g. react-redux with `mapStateToProps()` and `mapDispatchToProps()`) that enables you to connect your components to the state. These components have access to the Redux store. They are used to receive state or to alter the state. They are a specialized case of a container component in the presenter and container pattern when using components.

Concept Playground

```
View -> (mapDispatchToProps) -> Action -> Reducer(s) -> Store -> (mapStateToProp\
s) -> View
```

All other components are not aware of any local or sophisticated state management solution. They only receive props, except they have their own local state management (such as `this.state` and `this.setState()` in React).

Concept Playground

```
View -> Connected View (mapDispatchToProps) -> Action -> Reducer(s) -> Store -> \
Connected View (mapStateToProps) -> View
```

State can be received directly by operating on the state object or indirectly by selecting it with selectors.

Code Playground

```
// directly from state object
state.something;

// indirectly from state object via selector
const getSomething = (state) => state.something;
```

State can be altered by dispatching an action directly or by using an action creator that returns an action object.

Code Playground

```
// dispatching an action directly
dispatch({ type: 'ANY_TYPE', payload: anyPayload });

// dispatching an action indirectly via action creator
function doAnything(payload) {
  return {
    type: 'ANY_TYPE',
    payload,
  };
}

dispatch(doAnything(anyPayload));
```

In order to keep your state predictable and manageable in the reducers, you can apply techniques for an improved state structure. You can normalize your state to have always a single source of truth. That means you don't have to operate on duplicated entities, but only on one reference of the entity. In addition, it keeps the state flat. It is easier to manage only by using JavaScript spread operators for keeping it immutable.

Around these practical usages, you have learned several supporting techniques. There are tons of opinionated ways to organize your folders and files. The book showcased two of the main approaches, but they vary in their execution from developer to developer, team to team, or company to company. Nevertheless, you should always bear in mind to keep Redux at a top level. It is not used to manage the state of one single component. Instead it is used to wire dedicated components to the store in order to enable them to alter and to retrieve the state from it.

Coupling actions and reducers is fine, but always think twice when adding another action type. For instance, perhaps a action type could be reused in another reducer. When reusing action types, you avoid to end up with fat thunks when using Redux thunk. Instead of dispatching several actions, your thunk could dispatch only one abstract action that is reused in more than one reducer.

You have learned that you can plan your state management ahead. There are use cases where local state makes more sense than sophisticated state. Both can be used and should be used in a scaling application. By combining local state to the native local storage of the browser, you can give the user of your application an improved UX. In addition, you can plan the state ahead too. Think about view state and entity state and where it should live in your application. You can give your reducers difference domains as their ownership such as todoReducer, filterReducer and notificationReducer. However, once you have planned your state management and state, don't stick to it. When growing your application, always revisit those things to apply refactorings. That will help you to keep your state manageable, maintainable and predictable in the long run.

Hands On: Hacker News with Redux

In this chapter, you will be guided to build your own Hacker News[97] application with React and Redux. Hacker News is a platform to share news around the technology domain. It provides a public API[98] to retrieve their data. Some of you might have read the Road to learn React[99] where you have build a Hacker News application as well. In that book it was only plain React. Now you can experience the differences when using Redux with React in this book.

You are going to use create-react-app to setup your project. You can read the official documentation[100] to get to know how it works. After you have installed it, you simply start by choosing a project name for your application.

Command Line

```
create-react-app react-redux-hackernews
```

After the project was created for you, you can navigate into the project folder, open your editor and start the application.

Command Line

```
cd react-redux-hackernews
npm start
```

In your browser it should show the defaults that come with create-create-app.

Part 1: Project Organization

Before you familiarize yourself with the folder structure in this part, you will adapt it to your own needs. First, navigate into the *src/* folder and delete the boilerplate files that are not needed for the application.

Command Line: /

```
cd src
rm logo.svg App.js App.test.js App.css
```

Even the App component is removed, because you'll organize it in folders instead of in the top level *src/* folder. Now, from the *src/* folder, create the folders for an organized folder structure by a technical separation. It is up to you to refactor it later to a feature folder organization.

---

[97]https://news.ycombinator.com/

[98]https://hn.algolia.com/api

[99]https://www.robinwieruch.de/the-road-to-learn-react/

[100]https://github.com/facebookincubator/create-react-app

Command Line: src/

```
mkdir components reducers actions selectors store sagas api constants
```

Your folder structure should be similar to the following:

Folder Structure

```
-src/
--actions/
--api/
--components/
--constants/
--reducers/
--sagas/
--selectors/
--store/
--index.css
--index.js
```

Navigate in the *components/* folder and create the following files for your independent components. These are not all components yet. You will create more of them on your own for this application afterward.

Command Line: src/

```
cd components
touch App.js Stories.js Story.js App.css Stories.css Story.css
```

You can continue this way and create the remaining files to end up with the following folder structure.

Folder Structure

```
-src/
--actions/
--api/
--components/
---App.js
---App.css
---Stories.js
---Stories.css
---Story.js
```

```
---Story.css
--constants/
---actionTypes.js
--reducers/
---index.js
--sagas/
---index.js
--selectors/
--store/
---index.js
--index.css
--index.js
```

Now you have your foundation of folders and files for your React and Redux application. Except for the specific component files that you already have, everything else can be used as a blueprint, your own boilerplate, for any application using React and Redux. But only if it is separated by technical concerns. In a growing application, you might want to separate your folders by feature. You can find this part of the chapter in the GitHub repository[101].

Part 2: Plain React Components

In this part you will implement your plain React component architecture that only receives all necessary props from their parent components. These props can include callback functions that will enable interactions later on. The point is that the props don't reveal where they are coming from. They could be props themselves that are located in the parent component, state from the local state or even Redux state. The callback functions are plain functions too. Thus the components are not aware of using local state methods or Redux actions to alter the state.

In your entry point to React, where your root component gets rendered into the DOM, adjust the import of the App component by including the components folder in the path.

src/index.js
```
import React from 'react';
import ReactDOM from 'react-dom';
import App from './components/App';
import './index.css';


ReactDOM.render(<App />, document.getElementById('root'));
```

In the next step, you can come up with sample data that can be used in the React components. The sample data becomes the input of the App component. At a later point in time, this data will get fetched from the Hacker News API.

---

[101]https://github.com/rwieruch/react-redux-hackernews/tree/d5ab6a77653ee641d339c0a6a91c8444eff3f699

src/index.js

```
...

const stories = [
  {
    title: 'React',
    url: 'https://facebook.github.io/react/',
    author: 'Jordan Walke',
    num_comments: 3,
    points: 4,
    objectID: 0,
  }, {
    title: 'Redux',
    url: 'https://github.com/reactjs/redux',
    author: 'Dan Abramov, Andrew Clark',
    num_comments: 2,
    points: 5,
    objectID: 1,
  },
];

ReactDOM.render(
  <App stories={stories} />,
  document.getElementById('root')
);
```

The three components, App, Stories and Story, are not defined yet but you have already created the files. Let's define them component by component. First, the App component receives the sample stories from above as props and its only responsibility is to render the Stories component and to pass over the stories as props.

src/components/App.js

```
import React from 'react';
import './App.css';

import Stories from './Stories';

const App = ({ stories }) =>
  <div className="app">
    <Stories stories={stories} />
  </div>
```

```
export default App;
```

Second, the Stories component receives the stories as props and renders for each story a Story component. You may want to default to an empty array that the Stories component doesn't crash when the list of stories is null.

src/components/Stories.js

```
import React from 'react';
import './Stories.css';

import Story from './Story';

const Stories = ({ stories }) =>
  <div className="stories">
    {(stories || []).map(story =>
      <Story
        key={story.objectID}
        story={story}
      />
    )}
  </div>

export default Stories;
```

Third, the Story component renders a few properties of the story object. The story object gets already destructured from the props in the function signature. Furthermore the story object gets destructured as well.

src/components/Story.js

```
import React from 'react';
import './Story.css';

const Story = ({ story }) => {
  const {
    title,
    url,
    author,
    num_comments,
    points,
  } = story;
```

```
  return (
    <div className="story">
      <span>
        <a href={url}>{title}</a>
      </span>
      <span>{author}</span>
      <span>{num_comments}</span>
      <span>{points}</span>
    </div>
  );
}


export default Story;
```

You can start your application again with npm start on the command line. Both sample stories should be displayed in plain React. You can find this part of the chapter in the GitHub repository[102].

Part 3: Apply Styling

The application looks a bit dull without any styling. Therefore you can drop in some of your own styling or use the styling that's provided in this part. First, the application would need some general style that can be defined in the root style file.

src/index.css

```
body {
  color: #222;
  background: #f4f4f4;
  font: 400 14px CoreSans, Arial,sans-serif;
}

a {
  color: #222;
}

a:hover {
  text-decoration: underline;
}

ul, li {
```

[102]https://github.com/rwieruch/react-redux-hackernews/tree/f5843d2a06033cd045e6d0427993e30e289031a7

```css
    list-style: none;
    padding: 0;
    margin: 0;
}

input {
    padding: 10px;
    border-radius: 5px;
    outline: none;
    margin-right: 10px;
    border: 1px solid #dddddd;
}

button {
    padding: 10px;
    border-radius: 5px;
    border: 1px solid #dddddd;
    background: transparent;
    color: #808080;
    cursor: pointer;
}

button:hover {
    color: #222;
}

.button-inline {
    border-width: 0;
    background: transparent;
    color: inherit;
    text-align: inherit;
    -webkit-font-smoothing: inherit;
    padding: 0;
    font-size: inherit;
    cursor: pointer;
}

.button-active {
    border-radius: 0;
    border-bottom: 1px solid #38BB6C;
}
```

```css
*:focus {
  outline: none;
}
```

Second, the App component gets a few CSS classes:

src/components/App.css

```css
.app {
  margin: 20px;
}

.interactions, .error {
  text-align: center;
}
```

Third, the Stories component gets some style:

src/components/Stories.css

```css
.stories {
  margin: 20px 0;
}

.stories-header {
  display: flex;
  line-height: 24px;
  font-size: 16px;
  padding: 0 10px;
  justify-content: space-between;
}

.stories-header > span {
  overflow: hidden;
  text-overflow: ellipsis;
  padding: 0 5px;
}
```

And last but not least, the Story component will get styled too:

src/components/Story.css

```
.story {
  display: flex;
  line-height: 24px;
  white-space: nowrap;
  margin: 10px 0;
  padding: 10px;
  background: #ffffff;
  border: 1px solid #e3e3e3;
}

.story > span {
  overflow: hidden;
  text-overflow: ellipsis;
  padding: 0 5px;
}
```

When you start your application again, it seems more organized by its styling. But there is still something missing for displaying the stories properly. The columns for each story should be aligned and perhaps there should be a heading for each column. First, you can define an object to describe the columns.

src/components/Stories.js

```
import React from 'react';
import './Stories.css';

import Story from './Story';

const COLUMNS = {
  title: {
    label: 'Title',
    width: '40%',
  },
  author: {
    label: 'Author',
    width: '30%',
  },
  comments: {
    label: 'Comments',
    width: '10%',
  },
```

```
  points: {
    label: 'Points',
    width: '10%',
  },
  archive: {
    width: '10%',
  },
};


const Stories = ({ stories }) =>
  ...
```

The last column with the archive property name will not be used yet, but will be used in a later point in time. Second, you can pass this object to your Story component. Still the Stories component has access to the object to use it later on for the column headings.

src/components/Stories.js

```
const Stories = ({ stories }) =>
  <div className="stories">
    {(stories || []).map(story =>
      <Story
        key={story.objectID}
        story={story}
        columns={COLUMNS}
      />
    )}
  </div>
```

The Story component can use the columns object to style each displaying property of the story. It uses inline style to define the width of each column which comes from the object.

src/components/Story.js

```
const Story = ({ story, columns }) => {

  ...

  return (
    <div className="story">
      <span style={{ width: columns.title.width }}>
        <a href={url}>{title}</a>
      </span>
```

```
      <span style={{ width: columns.author.width }}>
        {author}
      </span>
      <span style={{ width: columns.comments.width }}>
        {num_comments}
      </span>
      <span style={{ width: columns.points.width }}>
        {points}
      </span>
      <span style={{ width: columns.archive.width }}>
      </span>
    </div>
  );
}
```

Last but not least, you can use the COLUMNS object to give your Stories component matching header columns. That's why the COLUMNS object got defined in the Stories component in the first place. Now, rather than doing it manually, as in the Story component, you will map over the object dynamically to render the header columns. Since it is an object, you have to turn it into an array of the property names first, and then access the object by its mapped keys again.

src/components/Stories.js

```
const Stories = ({ stories }) =>
  <div className="stories">
    <div className="stories-header">
      {Object.keys(COLUMNS).map(key =>
        <span
          key={key}
          style={{ width: COLUMNS[key].width }}
        >
          {COLUMNS[key].label}
        </span>
      )}
    </div>

    {(stories || []).map(story =>
      <Story
        key={story.objectID}
        story={story}
        columns={COLUMNS}
      />
```

```
  )}
</div>
```

You can extract the header columns as its own StoriesHeader component to keep your components well arranged and separated by concerns.

src/components/Stories.js

```
const Stories = ({ stories }) =>
  <div className="stories">
    <StoriesHeader columns={COLUMNS} />

    {(stories || []).map(story =>
      ...
    )}
  </div>

const StoriesHeader = ({ columns }) =>
  <div className="stories-header">
    {Object.keys(columns).map(key =>
      <span
        key={key}
        style={{ width: columns[key].width }}
      >
        {columns[key].label}
      </span>
    )}
  </div>
```

In this part, you have applied styling for your application and components. It should be in a representable state from a developer's point of view. You can find this part of the chapter in the GitHub repository[103].

Part 4: Archive a Story

Now you will add your first functionality: archiving a story. Therefore you will have to introduce Redux at some point to your application to manage the state of archived stories. I want to highly emphasize that it would work in plain React too. But for the sake of learning Redux, you will already use it at this point in time.

First, the archiving functionality can be passed down to the Story component from your React root component. In the beginning, it can be an empty function. The function will be replaced later when you will dispatch a Redux action.

---

[103]https://github.com/rwieruch/react-redux-hackernews/tree/6cb35b024abb59a2192c8ac0bb700046a700d470

src/index.js

```
...

ReactDOM.render(
  <App stories={stories} onArchive={() => {}} />,
  document.getElementById('root')
);
```

Second, you can pass it through your App and Stories components. These components don't use the function but only pass it to the Story component. You might already notice that this could be a potential refactoring later on, because the function gets passed from the root component through a few components only to reach a leaf component. It passes the App component:

src/components/App.js

```
const App = ({ stories, onArchive }) =>
  <div className="app">
    <Stories
      stories={stories}
      onArchive={onArchive}
    />
  </div>
```

And it passes the Stories component:

src/components/Stories.js

```
const Stories = ({ stories, onArchive }) =>
  <div className="stories">
    <StoriesHeader columns={COLUMNS} />

    {(stories || []).map(story =>
      <Story
        key={story.objectID}
        story={story}
        columns={COLUMNS}
        onArchive={onArchive}
      />
    )}
  </div>
```

Finally, you can use it in your Story component in a onClick handler of a button. The story objectID will be passed in the handler to identify the archived story.

src/components/Story.js

```
const Story = ({ story, columns, onArchive }) => {
  const {
    title,
    url,
    author,
    num_comments,
    points,
    objectID,
  } = story;

  return (
    <div className="story">
      ...
      <span style={{ width: columns.archive.width }}>
        <button
          type="button"
          className="button-inline"
          onClick={() => onArchive(objectID)}
        >
          Archive
        </button>
      </span>
    </div>
  );
}
```

A refactoring that you could already do would be to extract the button as a reusable component.

src/components/Story.js

```
const Story = ({ story, columns, onArchive }) => {
  ...

  return (
    <div className="story">
      ...
      <span style={{ width: columns.archive.width }}>
        <ButtonInline onClick={() => onArchive(objectID)}>
          Archive
        </ButtonInline>
      </span>
```

```
    </div>
  );
}

const ButtonInline = ({
  onClick,
  type = 'button',
  children
}) =>
  <button
    type={type}
    className="button-inline"
    onClick={onClick}
  >
    {children}
  </button>
```

You can make even another more abstract `Button` component that doesn't share the `button-inline` CSS class.

src/components/Story.js

```
...

const ButtonInline = ({
  onClick,
  type = 'button',
  children
}) =>
  <Button
    type={type}
    className="button-inline"
    onClick={onClick}
  >
    {children}
  </Button>

const Button = ({
  onClick,
  className,
  type = 'button',
  children
}) =>
```

```
<button
  type={type}
  className={className}
  onClick={onClick}
>
  {children}
</button>
```

Both button components should be extracted to a new file called *src/components/Button.js*, but exported so that at least the `ButtonInline` component can be reused in the `Story` component. You can find this part of the chapter in the GitHub repository[104]. Now, when you start your application again, the button to archive a story is there. But it doesn't work because it only receives a no-op (empty function) as property from your React root component. Later you will introduce a Redux action that can be dispatched from this function to archive a story.

Part 5: Introduce Redux: Store + First Reducer

This part will finally introduce Redux to manage the state of the (sample) stories instead of passing it directly into your component tree. Let's approach it step by step. First, you have to install Redux on the command line:

Command Line

```
npm install --save redux
```

Second, in the root entry point of React, you can import the Redux store. The store is not defined yet. Instead of using the sample stories, you will use the stories that are stored in the Redux store. Taken that the store only saves a list of stories as state, you can simply get the root state of the store and assume that it is the list of stories.

src/index.js

```
import React from 'react';
import ReactDOM from 'react-dom';
import App from './components/App';
import store from './store';
import './index.css';

ReactDOM.render(
  <App stories={store.getState()} onArchive={() => {}} />,
  document.getElementById('root')
);
```

---

[104]https://github.com/rwieruch/react-redux-hackernews/tree/55de13475aa9c2424b0fc00ce95dd4c5474c0473

Third, you have to create your Redux store instance in a separate file. It already takes a reducer that is not implemented yet. You will implement it in the next step.

src/store/index.js

```
import { createStore } from 'redux';
import storyReducer from '../reducers/story';

const store = createStore(
  storyReducer
);

export default store;
```

Fourth, in your *src/reducers/* folder you can create your first reducer: storyReducer. It can have the sample stories as initial state.

src/reducers/story.js

```
const INITIAL_STATE = [
  {
    title: 'React',
    url: 'https://facebook.github.io/react/',
    author: 'Jordan Walke',
    num_comments: 3,
    points: 4,
    objectID: 0,
  }, {
    title: 'Redux',
    url: 'https://github.com/reactjs/redux',
    author: 'Dan Abramov, Andrew Clark',
    num_comments: 2,
    points: 5,
    objectID: 1,
  },
];

function storyReducer(state = INITIAL_STATE, action) {
  switch(action.type) {
    default : return state;
  }
}

export default storyReducer;
```

Your application should work when you start it. It is using the state from the Redux store that is initialized in the storyReducer, because it is the only reducer in your application. There are no actions yet and no action is captured in the reducer yet. Even though there was no action dispatched, you can see that the Redux store runs through all its defined reducers to initialize its initial state in the store. The state gets visible through the Stories and Story components, because it is passed down from the React root entry point. You can find this part of the chapter in the GitHub repository[105].

Part 6: Two Reducers

You have used the Redux store and a reducer to define an initial state of sample stories and to retrieve this state for your component tree. But there is no state manipulation happening yet. In the following parts you are going to implement the archive functionality. When approaching this functionality, the simplest thing to do would be to remove the archived story from the list of stories in the storyReducer. But let's approach this from a different angle to have a greater impact in the long run. It could still be useful to have all stories in the end, but have a way to distinguish between them: stories and archived stories. Following this way, you would be able in the future to have a second component that shows the archived stories next to the available stories.

From an implementation point of view, the storyReducer will stay as it is for now. But you can introduce a second reducer, a archiveReducer, that keeps a list of references to the archived stories.

src/reducers/archive.js

```
const INITIAL_STATE = [];

function archiveReducer(state = INITIAL_STATE, action) {
  switch(action.type) {
    default : return state;
  }
}

export default archiveReducer;
```

You will implement the action to archive a story in a second. First, the Redux store in its instantiation needs to get both reducers now. It has to get the combined reducer. Let's pretend that the store can import the combined reducer from the entry file, the *reducers/index.js*, without worrying about the combining of the reducers yet.

---

[105]https://github.com/rwieruch/react-redux-hackernews/tree/5aafb21595541c21db778ad8825c97403e44b963

src/store/index.js

```
import { createStore } from 'redux';
import rootReducer from '../reducers';

const store = createStore(
  rootReducer
);

export default store;
```

Next you can combine both reducers in the file that is used by the Redux store to import the rootReducer.

src/reducers/index.js

```
import { combineReducers } from 'redux';
import storyReducer from './story';
import archiveReducer from './archive';

const rootReducer = combineReducers({
  storyState: storyReducer,
  archiveState: archiveReducer,
});

export default rootReducer;
```

Since your state is sliced up into two substates now, you have to adjust how you retrieve the stories from your store with the intermediate storyState. This is a crucial step, because it shows how a combined reducer slices up your state into substates.

src/index.js

```
ReactDOM.render(
  <App
    stories={store.getState().storyState}
    onArchive={() => {}}
  />,
  document.getElementById('root')
);
```

The application should show up the same stories as before when you start it. You can find this part of the chapter in the GitHub repository[106]. However, there is still no state manipulation happening, because no actions are involved yet. Finally in the next part you will dispatch your first action to archive a story.

Part 7: First Action

In this part, you will dispatch your first action to archive a story. The archive action needs to be captured in the new archiveReducer. It simply stores all archived stories by their id in a list. There is no need to duplicate the story entity, because you want to keep the law of a single source of truth. The initial state is an empty list, because no story is archived in the beginning. When archiving a story, all the previous ids in the state and the new archived id will be used in a new array. The JavaScript spread operator is used here.

src/reducers/archive.js

```
import { STORY_ARCHIVE } from '../constants/actionTypes';

const INITIAL_STATE = [];

const applyArchiveStory = (state, action) =>
  [ ...state, action.id ];

function archiveReducer(state = INITIAL_STATE, action) {
  switch(action.type) {
    case STORY_ARCHIVE : {
      return applyArchiveStory(state, action);
    }
    default : return state;
  }
}

export default archiveReducer;
```

The action type is already outsourced in a different file. This way it can be reused when dispatching the action from the Redux store.

---

[106]https://github.com/rwieruch/react-redux-hackernews/tree/f6d436fdfdab19296e473fbe7243690e830c1c2b

src/constants/actionTypes.js

```
export const STORY_ARCHIVE = 'STORY_ARCHIVE';
```

Last but not least, you can import the action type and dispatch the action in your root component where you had the empty function before.

src/reducers/archive.js

```
import React from 'react';
import ReactDOM from 'react-dom';
import App from './components/App';
import store from './store';
import { STORY_ARCHIVE } from './constants/actionTypes';
import './index.css';

ReactDOM.render(
  <App
    stories={store.getState().storyState}
    onArchive={id => store.dispatch({ type: STORY_ARCHIVE, id })}
  />,
  document.getElementById('root')
);
```

Now you dispatch the action directly without an action creator. You can find this part of the chapter in the GitHub repository[107]. When you start your application, it should still work, but nothing happens when you archive a story. The archived stories are not yet evaluated in the component tree. The `stories` prop that is passed to the `App` component still uses all the stories from the `storyState`.

Part 8: First Selector

You can use both substates, `storyState` and `archiveState` to derive the list of stories that are not archived. The deriving of those properties can happen in a selector. You can create your first selector that only returns the part of the stories that is not archived. The `archiveState` is the list of archived ids.

---

src/selectors/story.js

```
const isNotArchived = archivedIds => story =>
  archivedIds.indexOf(story.objectID) === -1;

const getReadableStories = ({ storyState, archiveState }) =>
  storyState.filter(isNotArchived(archiveState));

export {
  getReadableStories,
};
```

The selector makes heavily use of JavaScript ES6 arrow functions, JavaScript ES6 destructuring and a higher-order function: isNotArchived(). If you are not used to JavaScript ES6, don't feel intimidated by it. It is only a way to express these functions more concise. In plain JavaScript ES5 it would look like the following:

src/selectors/story.js

```
function isNotArchived(archivedIds) {
  return function (story) {
    return archivedIds.indexOf(story.objectID) === -1;
  };
}

function getReadableStories({ storyState, archiveState }) {
  return storyState.filter(isNotArchived(archiveState));
}

export {
  getReadableStories,
};
```

Last but not least, you can use the selector to compute the not archived stories instead of retrieving the whole list of stories from the store directly.

src/index.js

```
import React from 'react';
import ReactDOM from 'react-dom';
import App from './components/App';
import store from './store';
import { getReadableStories } from './selectors/story';
import { STORY_ARCHIVE } from './constants/actionTypes';
import './index.css';

ReactDOM.render(
  <App
    stories={getReadableStories(store.getState())}
    onArchive={id => store.dispatch({ type: STORY_ARCHIVE, id })}
  />,
  document.getElementById('root')
);
```

You can find this part of the chapter in the GitHub repository[108]. When you start your application, nothing happens again when you archive a story. Even though you are using the readable stories now. That's because there is no re-rendering of the view in place to update it.

Part 9: Re-render View

In this part, you will update the view layer to reflect the correct state that is used from the Redux store. When an action dispatches, the state in the Redux store gets updated. However, the component tree in React doesn't update, because no one subscribed to the Redux store yet. In the first attempt, you are going to wire up Redux and React naively and re-render the whole component tree on each updatea as you have done before in another application from this book.

src/index.js

```
...

function render() {
  ReactDOM.render(
    <App
      stories={getReadableStories(store.getState())}
      onArchive={id => store.dispatch({ type: STORY_ARCHIVE, id })}
    />,
    document.getElementById('root')
```

---

[108]https://github.com/rwieruch/react-redux-hackernews/tree/5e3338d3ffff924b7a12eccb691365fd11cb5aed

```
    );
}

store.subscribe(render);
render();
```

Now the components will re-render once you archive a story, because the state in the Redux store updates and the subscription will run to render again the whole component tree. In addition, you render the component only once when the application starts. Congratulations, you dispatched your first action, selected derived properties from the state and updated your component tree by subscribing it to the Redux store. That took longer as expected, didn't it? However, now most of the Redux and React infrastructure is in place to be more efficient when introducing new features. You can find this part of the chapter in the GitHub repository[109].

Part 10: First Middleware

In this part, you will introduce your first middleware to the Redux store. In a scaling application it becomes often a problem to track state updates. Often you don't notice when an action is dispatched, because too many actions get involved and a bunch of them might get triggered implicitly. Therefore you can use the redux-logger[110] middleware in your Redux store to console.log() every action, the previous state and the next state, automatically to your developers console when dispatching an action. First, you have to install the neat middleware library.

Command Line

```
npm install --save redux-logger
```

Second, you can use it as middleware in your Redux store initialization.

src/store/index.js

```
import { createStore, applyMiddleware } from 'redux';
import { createLogger } from 'redux-logger';
import rootReducer from '../reducers';

const logger = createLogger();

const store = createStore(
  rootReducer,
  undefined,
```

[109]https://github.com/rwieruch/react-redux-hackernews/tree/286c04354fcab639ebd60ac2430ad939ce107365
[110]https://github.com/evgenyrodionov/redux-logger

```
applyMiddleware(logger)
);

export default store;
```

That's it. Every time you dispatch an action now, for instance when archiving a story, you will see the logging in the developer console in your browser. You can find this part of the chapter in the GitHub repository[111].

Part 11: First Action Creator

The action you are dispatching is a plain action object. However, you might want to reuse it in a later point in time. Action creators are not mandatory, but they keep your Redux architecture organized. In order to stay organized, let's define your first action creator. First, you have to define the action creator that takes a story id, to identify the archiving story, in a new file.

src/actions/archive.js

```
import { STORY_ARCHIVE } from '../constants/actionTypes';

const doArchiveStory = id => ({
  type: STORY_ARCHIVE,
  id,
});

export {
  doArchiveStory,
};
```

Second, you can use it in your root component. Instead of dispatching the action object directly, you can create an action by using its action creator.

---

[111]https://github.com/rwieruch/react-redux-hackernews/tree/652e6419e2a872ba2d1dd65465006b13f0799c4f

src/index.js

```
import React from 'react';
import ReactDOM from 'react-dom';
import App from './components/App';
import store from './store';
import { getReadableStories } from './selectors/story';
import { doArchiveStory } from './actions/archive';
import './index.css';

function render() {
  ReactDOM.render(
    <App
      stories={getReadableStories(store.getState())}
      onArchive={id => store.dispatch(doArchiveStory(id))}
    />,
    document.getElementById('root')
  );
}

...
```

The application should operate as before when you start it. But this time you have used an action creator rather than dispatching an action object directly. You can find this part of the chapter in the GitHub repository[112].

Part 12: Connect React with Redux

In this part, you will connect React and Redux in a more sophisticated way. The whole component tree re-renders every time when the state changes now. However, you might want to wire up components independently with the Redux store. In addition, you don't want to re-render the whole component tree, but only the components where the state or props have changed. Let's change this by using the react-redux[113] library that connects both worlds.

Command Line

```
npm install --save react-redux
```

You can use the Provider component, which makes the Redux store available to all components below, in your React root entry point.

---

[112]https://github.com/rwieruch/react-redux-hackernews/tree/4cc5e995d63fd935a2e335b0a4946a1811c04202

[113]https://github.com/reactjs/react-redux

src/index.js

```
import React from 'react';
import ReactDOM from 'react-dom';
import { Provider } from 'react-redux';
import App from './components/App';
import store from './store';
import './index.css';

ReactDOM.render(
  <Provider store={store}>
    <App />
  </Provider>,
  document.getElementById('root')
);
```

Notice that the render method isn't used in a Redux store subscription anymore. No one subscribes to the Redux store and the App component isn't receiving any props. In addition, the App component is only rendering a component and doesn't pass any props.

src/components/App.js

```
import React from 'react';
import './App.css';

import Stories from './Stories';

const App = () =>
  <div className="app">
    <Stories />
  </div>

export default App;
```

But who gives the props to the Stories component then? This component is the first component that needs to know about the list of stories, because it has to display it. The solution is to upgrade the Stories component to a connected component. It should be connected to the state layer. So, instead of only exporting the plain Stories component:

src/components/Stories.js

```
...

export default Stories;
```

You can export the connected component that has access to the Redux store:

src/components/Stories.js

```
import { connect } from 'react-redux';
import { doArchiveStory } from '../actions/archive';
import { getReadableStories } from '../selectors/story';

...

const mapStateToProps = state => ({
  stories: getReadableStories(state),
});

const mapDispatchToProps = dispatch => ({
  onArchive: id => dispatch(doArchiveStory(id)),
});

export default connect(
  mapStateToProps,
  mapDispatchToProps
)(Stories);
```

The Stories component is a connected component now and is the only component that has access to the Redux store. It receives the stories from the state in mapStateToProps() and a function that triggers the dispatching of an action to archive a story in mapDispatchToProps(). The application should work again, but this time with a sophisticated connection between Redux and React. You can find this part of the chapter in the GitHub repository[114].

Part 13: Lift Connection

It is no official term (yet), but you can lift the connection between React and Redux. For instance, you could lift the connection from the Stories component to another component. But you need the list of stories to map over them in the Stories component. However, what about the onArchive()

---

[114]https://github.com/rwieruch/react-redux-hackernews/tree/88072e9b62230f59ffa83a5ddd06ceda6bf75fe4

function? It is not used in the Stories component, but only in the Story component and only passed via the Stories component. Thus you could lift the connection partly. The stories would stay in the Stories component, but the onArchive() function could live in the Story component.

First, you remove the onArchive() function for the Stories component and remove the mapDispatchToProps() as well. It will be used later on in the Story component.

src/components/Stories.js

```
. . .


const Stories = ({ stories }) =>
  <div className="stories">
    <StoriesHeader columns={COLUMNS} />

    {(stories || []).map(story =>
      <Story
        key={story.objectID}
        story={story}
        columns={COLUMNS}
      />
    )}
  </div>


. . .


const mapStateToProps = state => ({
  stories: getReadableStories(state),
});

export default connect(
  mapStateToProps
)(Stories);
```

Now you can connect the Story component instead whereas you have two connected components afterward.

src/components/Story.js

```
import { connect } from 'react-redux';
import { doArchiveStory } from '../actions/archive';

...

const mapDispatchToProps = dispatch => ({
  onArchive: id => dispatch(doArchiveStory(id)),
});

export default connect(
  null,
  mapDispatchToProps
)(Story);
```

With this refactoring step in your mind, you can always lift your connections to the Redux store in your view layer depending on the needs of the components. Does the component need state from the Redux store? Does the component need to alter the state in the Redux store via dispatching an action? You are in full control of where you want to use connected components (a subset of container components) and where you want to keep your components as presenter components. You can find this part of the chapter in the GitHub repository[115].

Part 14: Interacting with an API

Implementing applications with sample data can be dull. It is way more exciting to interact with a real API - in this case the Hacker News API[116]. Even though, as you have learned, you can have asynchronous actions without any asynchronous action library, this application will introduce Redux Saga as asynchronous action library to deal with side-effects such as fetching data from a third-party platform.

Command Line: /

```
npm install --save redux-saga
```

First, you can introduce a root saga in your entry point file to sagas. It can be similar seen to the combined root reducer, because in the end the Redux store expects one root saga for its creation. Basically the root saga watches all saga activated actions by using effects such as takeEvery().

---

[115]https://github.com/rwieruch/react-redux-hackernews/tree/779d52fc85ecfbaf5a821cbbae384aac962e76a7
[116]https://hn.algolia.com/api

src/sagas/index.js

```
import { takeEvery, all } from 'redux-saga/effects';
import { STORIES_FETCH } from '../constants/actionTypes';
import { handleFetchStories } from './story';

function *watchAll() {
  yield all([
    takeEvery(STORIES_FETCH, handleFetchStories),
  ])
}

export default watchAll;
```

Second, the root saga can be used in the Redux store middleware when initializing the saga middleware. It is used in the middleware, but also needs to be run in a saga.run() method.

src/store/index.js

```
import { createStore, applyMiddleware } from 'redux';
import { createLogger } from 'redux-logger';
import createSagaMiddleware from 'redux-saga';
import rootReducer from '../reducers';
import rootSaga from '../sagas';

const logger = createLogger();
const saga = createSagaMiddleware();

const store = createStore(
  rootReducer,
  undefined,
  applyMiddleware(saga, logger)
);

saga.run(rootSaga);

export default store;
```

Third, you can introduce the new action type in your constants that will activate the saga. However, you can already introduce a second action type that will later on - when the request succeeds - add the stories in your storyReducer to the Redux store. Basically you have one action to activate the side-effect that is handled with Redux Saga and one action that stores the result of the side-effect in the Redux store.

src/constants/actionTypes.js

```
export const STORY_ARCHIVE = 'STORY_ARCHIVE';
export const STORIES_FETCH = 'STORIES_FETCH';
export const STORIES_ADD = 'STORIES_ADD';
```

Fourth, you can implement the story saga that encapsulates the API request. It uses the native fetch API of the browser to retrieve the stories from the Hacker News API endpoint. In your `handleFetchStories()` generator function, that is used in your root saga, you can use the `yield` statement to write asynchronous code as it would be synchronous code. As long as the promise from the Hacker News request doesn't resolve (or reject), the next line of code after the `yield` state will not be evaluated. When you finally have the result from the API request, you can use the `put()` effect to dispatch another action.

src/sagas/story.js

```
import { call, put } from 'redux-saga/effects';
import { doAddStories } from '../actions/story';

const HN_BASE_URL = 'http://hn.algolia.com/api/v1/search?query=';

const fetchStories = query =>
  fetch(HN_BASE_URL + query)
    .then(response => response.json());

function* handleFetchStories(action) {
  const { query } = action;
  const result = yield call(fetchStories, query);
  yield put(doAddStories(result.hits));
}

export {
  handleFetchStories,
};
```

In the fifth step, you need to define both actions creators: the first one that activates the side-effect to fetch stories by a search term and the second one that adds the fetched stories to your Redux store.

src/actions/story.js

```
import {
  STORIES_ADD,
  STORIES_FETCH,
} from '../constants/actionTypes';

const doAddStories = stories => ({
  type: STORIES_ADD,
  stories,
});

const doFetchStories = query => ({
  type: STORIES_FETCH,
  query,
});

export {
  doAddStories,
  doFetchStories,
};
```

Only the second action needs to be intercepted in your storyReducer to store the stories. The first action is only used to activate the saga in your root saga. Don't forget to remove the sample stories in your reducers, because they are coming from the API now.

src/reducers/story.js

```
import { STORIES_ADD } from '../constants/actionTypes';

const INITIAL_STATE = [];

const applyAddStories = (state, action) =>
  action.stories;

function storyReducer(state = INITIAL_STATE, action) {
  switch(action.type) {
    case STORIES_ADD : {
      return applyAddStories(state, action);
    }
    default : return state;
  }
}
```

```
export default storyReducer;
```

Now, everything is setup from a Redux and Redux Saga perspective. As last step, only one component from the view layer needs to activate the STORIES_FETCH action. This action is intercepted in the saga, fetches the stories in a side-effect, and stores them in the Redux store with the other STORIES_ADD action. Therefore, in your App component, you can introduce the new SearchStories component.

src/components/App.js

```
import React from 'react';
import './App.css';

import Stories from './Stories';
import SearchStories from './SearchStories';

const App = () =>
  <div className="app">
    <div className="interactions">
      <SearchStories />
    </div>
    <Stories />
  </div>

export default App;
```

The SearchStories component will be a connected component. It is the next step to implement this component. First, you start with a plain React component that has a form, input field and button.

src/components/SearchStories.js

```
import React, { Component } from 'react';
import Button from './Button';

class SearchStories extends Component {
  constructor(props) {
    super(props);

    this.state = {
      query: '',
    };
  }
```

```
render() {
  return (
    <form onSubmit={this.onSubmit}>
      <input
        type="text"
        value={this.state.query}
        onChange={this.onChange}
      />
      <Button type="submit">
        Search
      </Button>
    </form>
  );
}
}


export default SearchStories;
```

There are two missing class methods: onChange() and onSubmit(). Let's introduce them to make the component complete.

src/components/SearchStories.js

```
...

const applyQueryState = query => () => ({
  query
});

class SearchStories extends Component {
  constructor(props) {
    ...

    this.onChange = this.onChange.bind(this);
    this.onSubmit = this.onSubmit.bind(this);
  }

  onSubmit(event) {
    const { query } = this.state;
    if (query) {
      this.props.onFetchStories(query)

      this.setState(applyQueryState(''));
```

```
    }

    event.preventDefault();
  }

  onChange(event) {
    const { value } = event.target;
    this.setState(applyQueryState(value));
  }

  render() {
    ...
  }
}


export default SearchStories;
```

The component should work on its own now. It only receives one function from the outside via its props: onFetchStories(). This function will dispatch an action to activate the saga that fetches the stories from the Hacker News platform. You would have to connect the SearchStories component to make the dispatch functionality available.

src/components/SearchStories.js

```
import React, { Component } from 'react';
import { connect } from 'react-redux';
import { doFetchStories } from '../actions/story';
import Button from './Button';


...


const mapDispatchToProps = (dispatch) => ({
  onFetchStories: query => dispatch(doFetchStories(query)),
});

export default connect(
  null,
  mapDispatchToProps
)(SearchStories);
```

Start your application again and try to search for stories such as "React" or "Redux". It should work now. The connect component dispatches an action that activates the saga. The side-effect of the saga is the fetching process of the stories by search term from the Hacker News API. Once the request succeeds, another action gets dispatched and captured in the storyReducer to finally store the stories. When using Redux Saga, it is essential to wrap your head around the subject that actions can be used to activate sagas but doesn't need to be evaluated in a reducer. It often happens that another action which is dispatched within the saga is evaluated by the reducers. You can find this part of the chapter in the GitHub repository[117].

Part 15: Separation of API

There is one refactoring step that you could apply. It would improve the separation between API functionalities and sagas. You would extract the API call from the story saga into an own API folder. Afterward, other sagas can make use of these API requests too. First, extract the functionality from the saga and instead import it.

src/sagas/story.js

```
import { call, put } from 'redux-saga/effects';
import { doAddStories } from '../actions/story';
import { fetchStories } from '../api/story';

function* handleFetchStories(action) {
  const { query } = action;
  const result = yield call(fetchStories, query);
  yield put(doAddStories(result.hits));
}

export {
  handleFetchStories,
};
```

And second, use it in an own dedicated API file.

---

src/api/story.js

```
const HN_BASE_URL = 'http://hn.algolia.com/api/v1/search?query=';

const fetchStories = query =>
  fetch(HN_BASE_URL + query)
    .then(response => response.json());

export {
  fetchStories,
};
```

Great, you have separated the API functionality from the saga. This way you made your API functions reusable to more than one saga. You can find this part of the chapter in the GitHub repository[118].

Part 16: Error Handling

So far, you are making a request to the Hacker News API and display the retrieved stories in your React components. But what happens when an error occurs? Nothing will show up when you search for stories. In order to give your end-user a great user experience, you could add error handling to your application. Let's do it by introducing an action that can allocate an error state in the Redux store.

src/constants/actionTypes.js

```
export const STORY_ARCHIVE = 'STORY_ARCHIVE';
export const STORIES_FETCH = 'STORIES_FETCH';
export const STORIES_FETCH_ERROR = 'STORIES_FETCH_ERROR';
export const STORIES_ADD = 'STORIES_ADD';
```

In the second step, you would need an action creator that keeps an error object in its payload and can be caught in a reducer later on.

---

[118]https://github.com/rwieruch/react-redux-hackernews/tree/b6a6e59af71613471a50c9366c4c4e107e00b66f

src/actions/story.js

```
import {
  STORIES_ADD,
  STORIES_FETCH,
  STORIES_FETCH_ERROR,
} from '../constants/actionTypes';

...

const doFetchErrorStories = error => ({
  type: STORIES_FETCH_ERROR,
  error,
});

export {
  doAddStories,
  doFetchStories,
  doFetchErrorStories,
};
```

The action can be called in your story saga now. Redux Saga, because of its generators, uses try and catch statements for error handling. Every time you would get an error in your try block, you would end up in the catch block to do something with the error object. In this case, you can dispatch your new action to store the error state in your Redux store.

src/sagas/story.js

```
import { call, put } from 'redux-saga/effects';
import { doAddStories, doFetchErrorStories } from '../actions/story';
import { fetchStories } from '../api/story';

function* handleFetchStories(action) {
  const { query } = action;

  try {
    const result = yield call(fetchStories, query);
    yield put(doAddStories(result.hits));
  } catch (error) {
    yield put(doFetchErrorStories(error));
  }
}
```

```
export {
  handleFetchStories,
};
```

Last but not least, a reducer needs to deal with the new action type. The best place to keep it would be next to the stories. The story reducer keeps only a list of stories so far, but you could change it to manage a complex object that holds the list of stories and an error object.

src/reducers/story.js

```
import { STORIES_ADD } from '../constants/actionTypes';

const INITIAL_STATE = {
  stories: [],
  error: null,
};

const applyAddStories = (state, action) => ({
  stories: action.stories,
  error: null,
});

function storyReducer(state = INITIAL_STATE, action) {
  switch(action.type) {
    case STORIES_ADD : {
      return applyAddStories(state, action);
    }
    default : return state;
  }
}

export default storyReducer;
```

Now you can introduce the second action type in the reducer. It would allocate the error object in the state but keeps the list of stories empty.

src/reducers/story.js

```
import {
  STORIES_ADD,
  STORIES_FETCH_ERROR,
} from '../constants/actionTypes';

...

const applyFetchErrorStories = (state, action) => ({
  stories: [],
  error: action.error,
});

function storyReducer(state = INITIAL_STATE, action) {
  switch(action.type) {
    case STORIES_ADD : {
      return applyAddStories(state, action);
    }
    case STORIES_FETCH_ERROR : {
      return applyFetchErrorStories(state, action);
    }
    default : return state;
  }
}

export default storyReducer;
```

In your story selector, you would have to change the structure of the story state. The story state isn't anymore a mere list of stories but a complex object with a list of stories and an error object. In addition, you could add a second selector to select the error object. It will be used later on in a component.

src/selectors/story.js

```
...

const getReadableStories = ({ storyState, archiveState }) =>
  storyState.stories.filter(isNotArchived(archiveState));

const getFetchError = ({ storyState }) =>
  storyState.error;
```

```
export {
  getReadableStories,
  getFetchError,
};
```

Last but not least, in your component you can retrieve the error object in your connect higher-order component and display with React's conditional rendering[119] an error message in case of an error in the state.

src/components/Stories.js

```
...
import {
  getReadableStories,
  getFetchError,
} from '../selectors/story';

...

const Stories = ({ stories, error }) =>
  <div className="stories">
    <StoriesHeader columns={COLUMNS} />

    { error && <p className="error">Something went wrong ...</p> }

    {(stories || []).map(story =>
      ...
    )}
  </div>

...

const mapStateToProps = state => ({
  stories: getReadableStories(state),
  error: getFetchError(state),
});

...
```

In your browser in the developer console, you can simulate being offline. You can try it and see that an error message shows up when searching for stories. When you go online again and search for

---

[119]https://www.robinwieruch.de/conditional-rendering-react/

stories, the error message should disappear. Instead a list of stories displays again. You can find this part of the chapter in the GitHub repository[120].

Part 17: Testing

Every application in production should be tested. Therefore, the next step could be to add a couple of tests to your application. The chapter will only cover a handful of tests to demonstrate testing in Redux. You could add more of them on your own. However, the chapter will not test your view layer, because this is covered in "The Road to learn React".

Since you have set up your application with create-react-app, it already comes with Jest[121] to test your application. You can give a filename the prefix *test* to include it in your test suite. Once you run npm test on the command line, all included tests will get executed. The following files were not created for you, thus you would have to create them on your own.

First, let's create a test file for the story reducer. As you have learned, a reducer gets a previous state and an action as input and returns a new state. It is a pure function and thus it should be simple to test because it has no side-effects.

src/reducers/story.test.js

```
import storyReducer from './story';

describe('story reducer', () => {
  it('adds stories to the story state', () => {
    const stories = ['a', 'b', 'c'];

    const action = {
      type: 'STORIES_ADD',
      stories,
    };

    const previousState = { stories: [], error: null };
    const expectedNewState = { stories, error: null };

    const newState = storyReducer(previousState, action);

    expect(newState).toEqual(expectedNewState);;
  });
});
```

---

[120]https://github.com/rwieruch/react-redux-hackernews/tree/a1f6a885357a891b5e94ade90728a1f2d3d1dbb9

[121]https://facebook.github.io/jest/

Basically you created the necessary inputs for your reducer and the expected output. Then you can compare both in your expectation. It depends on your test philosophy whether you create the action again in the file or import your action creator that you already have from your application. In this case, an action was used.

In order to verify that your previous state isn't mutated when creating the new state, because Redux embraces immutable data structures, you could use a neat helper library that freezes your state.

Command Line: /

```
npm install --save-dev deep-freeze
```

In this case, it can be used to freeze the previous state.

src/reducers/story.test.js

```
import deepFreeze from 'deep-freeze';
import storyReducer from './story';

describe('story reducer', () => {
  it('adds stories to the story state', () => {
    const stories = ['a', 'b', 'c'];

    const action = {
      type: 'STORIES_ADD',
      stories,
    };

    const previousState = { stories: [], error: null };
    const expectedNewState = { stories, error: null };

    deepFreeze(previousState);
    const newState = storyReducer(previousState, action);

    expect(newState).toEqual(expectedNewState);;
  });
});
```

Now, every time you would mutate accidentally your previous state in the reducer, an error in your test would show up. It is up to you to add two more tests for the story reducer. One test could verify that an error object is set when an error occurs and another test that verifies that the error object is set to null when stories are successfully added to the state.

Second, you can add a test for your selectors. Let's demonstrate it with your story selector. Since the selector function is a pure function again, you can easily test it with an input and an expected output. You would have to define your global state and use the selector the retrieve an expected substate.

src/selectors/story.test.js

```
import { getReadableStories } from './story';

describe('story selector', () => {
  it('retrieves readable stories', () => {
    const storyState = {
      error: null,
      stories: [
        { objectID: '1', title: 'foo' },
        { objectID: '2', title: 'bar' },
      ],
    };
    const archiveState = ['1'];
    const state = { storyState, archiveState }

    const expectedReadableStories = [{ objectID: '2', title: 'bar' }];
    const readableStories = getReadableStories(state);

    expect(readableStories).toEqual(expectedReadableStories);;
  });
});
```

That's it. Your Redux state is a combination of the storyState and the archiveState. When both are defined, you already have your global state. The selector is used to retrieve a substate from the global state. Thus you would only have to check if all the readable stories that were not archived are retrieved by the selector.

Third, you can add a test for your action creators. An action creator only gets a payload and returns an action object. The expected action object can be tested.

src/actions/story.test.js

```
import { doAddStories } from './story';

describe('story action', () => {
  it('adds stories', () => {
    const stories = ['a', 'b'];

    const expectedAction = {
      type: 'STORIES_ADD',
```

```
    stories,
  };
  const action = doAddStories(stories);

  expect(action).toEqual(expectedAction);;
  });
});
```

As you can see, testing reducers, selectors and action creators follows always a similar pattern. Due to the functions being pure functions, you can focus on the input and output of these functions. In the previous examples all three test cases were strictly decoupled. However, you could also decide to import your action creator in your reducer test avoid creating a hard coded action. You can find this part of the chapter in the GitHub repository[122].

Final Words

Implementing this application could go on infinitely. I would have plenty of features in my head that I would want to add to it. What about you? Can you imagine to continue building this application? From a technical perspective, things that were taught in this book, everything is set up to give you the perfect starting point. However, there were more topics in this book that you could apply. For instance, you could normalize your incoming stories from the API before they reach the Redux store. The following list should give you an idea about potential next steps:

- Normalization: The data that comes from the Hacker News API could be normalized before it reaches the reducer and finally the Redux store. You could use the normalizr library that was introduced earlier in the book. It might be not necessary yet to normalize your state, but in a growing application you would normalize your data eventually. The data would be normalized between fetching the data and sending it via an action creator to the reducers.
- Local State: So far you have only used Redux. But what about mixing local state into the application? Could you imagine a use case for it? For instance, you would be able to distinguish between readable and archived stories in your application. There could be a toggle, that is true or false in your Stories component as local state, that decides whether the component shows readable or archived stories. Depending on the toggle in your view layer, you would retrieve either readable or archived stories via selectors from your Redux store and display them.
- React Router: Similar to the previous step, using a toggle to show archived and readable stories, you could add a view layer Router to display these different stories on two routes. It could be React Router when using React as your view layer. All of this is possible, because fortunately you don't delete stories when archiving them from your Redux store, but keep a list of archived stories in a separate substate.

---

[122]https://github.com/rwieruch/react-redux-hackernews/tree/d1fcb31b7a1b1602069718941844d08c21583607

- Paginated Data: The response from the Hacker News API doesn't only return the list of stories. It returns a paginated list of stories with a page property. You could use the page property to fetch more stories with the same search term. The list component in React could be a paginated list[123] or infinite scroll list[124].
- Caching: You could cache the incoming data from the Hacker News API in your Redux store. It could be cached by search term. When you search for a search term twice, the Redux store could be used, when a result by search term is already in place. Otherwise a request to the Hacker News API would be made. In the Road to learn React[125] readers create a cache in React's local state. However, the same can be done in a Redux store.
- Local Storage: You already keep track of your archived stories in the Redux store. You could introduce the native local storage of the browser, as you have seen in the plain React chapters, to keep this state persistent. When a user loads the application, there could be a lookup in the local storage for archived stories. If there are archived stories, they could be rehydrated into the Redux store. When a story gets archived, it would be dehydrated into the local storage too. That way you would keep the list of archived stories in your Redux store and local storage in sync, but would add a persistent layer to it when an user closes your application and comes back later to it.

As you can see, there are a multitude of features you could implement or techniques you could make use of. Be curious and apply these on your own. After you come up with your own implementations, I am keen to see them. Feel free to reach out to me on Twitter[126].

---

[123]https://www.robinwieruch.de/react-paginated-list/

[124]https://www.robinwieruch.de/react-infinite-scroll/

[125]https://www.robinwieruch.de/the-road-to-learn-react/

[126]https://twitter.com/rwieruch

Redux Ecosystem Outline

After learning the basics and advanced techniques in Redux and applying them on your own in an application, you are ready to explore the Redux ecosystem. The Redux ecosystem is huge and cannot be covered in one book. However, this chapter attempts to outline different paths you can take to explore the world of Redux. Apart from outlining these different paths, a couple of topics will be revisited as well to give you a richer toolset when using Redux.

Before you are left alone with the last chapter covering Redux, I want to make you aware of this repository[127] by Mark Erikson. It is a categorized list of Redux related add-ons, libraries and articles. If you get stuck at some point, want to find a solution for your problem, or are just curious about the ecosystem, check out the repository. Otherwise, I encourage you to join the official Slack Group[128] for further recommendations.

---

[127]https://github.com/markerikson/redux-ecosystem-links

[128]https://slack-the-road-to-learn-react.wieruch.com/

Redux DevTools

The Redux DevTools are essential for many developers when implementing Redux applications. It improves the Redux development workflow by offering a rich set of features such as inspecting the state and action payload, time traveling and realtime optimizations.

How does it work? Basically, you have two choices to use the Redux DevTools. Either you integrate it directly into your project by using its node package with npm or you install the official browser extension. While the former comes with an implementation setup in your application, the latter can simply be installed for your browser without changing your implementation.

The most obvious feature is to inspect actions and state. Rather than using the redux-logger[129], you can use the Redux DevTools to get insights into these information. You can follow each state change by inspecting the action and the state.

Another great feature is the possibility to time travel. In Redux you dispatch actions and travel from one state to another state. The Redux DevTools enable you to travel back in time by reverting actions. For instance, that way you wouldn't need to reload your browser anymore to follow a set of actions to get to a specific application state. You could simply alter the actions in between by using the Redux DevTools. You can trace back what action led to which state.

In addition, you can persist your Redux state when doing page reloads with Redux DevTools. That way, you don't need to perform all the necessary actions to get to a specific state anymore. You simply reload the page and keep the same application state. This enables you to debug your application when having one specific application state.

However, there are more neat features that you might enjoy while developing a Redux application. You can find all information about the Redux DevTools in the official repository[130].

---

[129]https://github.com/evgenyrodionov/redux-logger
[130]https://github.com/gaearon/redux-devtools

Connect Revisited

In one of the previous chapters, you have connected your view layer to your state layer with react-redux[131]. There you have used the provider pattern in React to make the state accessible to your entire view layer.

The connect higher-order components enabled you to wire the Redux store to any component. The most often used two arguments are mapStateToProps() and mapDispatchToProps() for the connect higher-order component. While the former gives access to the state, the latter gives access to actions to be dispatched for manipulating the state.

However, connect has two more optional arguments that shouldn't stay uncovered in this book.

The third argument is called mergeProps(). As arguments it gets the result from mapStateToProps(), mapDispatchToProps() and the parent props: mergeProps(stateProps, dispatchProps, ownProps). The function returns props as an object to the wrapped component. Basically, it gives you an intermediate layer to mix up stateProps and dispatchProps before they reach the wrapped component. However, it is rarely used. Often, when mixing up state and actions in this layer, it is associated with a bad state architecture. You should ask yourself if something else can be changed to avoid this intermediate layer.

The fourth argument is called options. It is an object to configure the connect higher-order component. It comes with these additional properties: pure, areStatesEqual(), areOwnPropsEqual(), areMergedPropsEqual(). How does it work altogether? When the first argument, the pure property, is set to true, the connect higher-order component will avoid re-rendering the view and avoids the calls to its arguments mapStateToProps(), mapDispatchToProps() and mergeProps(). But only when the equality checks of areStatesEqual(), areOwnPropsEqual(), areMergedPropsEqual() remain equal based on their respective equality checks. These equality checks are performed on the previous state and props and updated state and props. These equality checks can be modified in the options areStatesEqual, areOwnPropsEqual, areMergedPropsEqual. Otherwise they have a default equality check.

After all, the options are a pure performance optimization. It is not often used when developing Redux applications. Basically, you can set the pure property to true to avoid re-renderings and other argument evaluations of the connect higher-order component. But it comes with certain default equality checks that can be configured. In addition, the underlying assumption is that the wrapped component is a pure component and doesn't rely on any other side-effect data.

If you want to read up the connect higher-order component again, you can checkout the official repository of react-redux[132] and look for the connect chapter.

---

[131]https://github.com/reactjs/react-redux

[132]https://github.com/reactjs/react-redux

Concise Actions and Reducers

Redux made state management predictable with clear constraints. Yet, these constraints come with a lot of code to manage actions and reducers. There are people who argue that writing Redux code is verbose. That's why there exist utility libraries on top of Redux to reduce the boilerplate code. One of them is called redux-actions[133].

The library attempts to make your actions and reducers concise. It comes with three methods: createAction(), handleAction() and combineActions(). The book will give you a brief overview of the former two methods.

The createAction() method is a utility for action creators. To be more specific, the method should be named: createActionCreator(). The only required argument for the method is an action type.

Code Playground

```
import { createAction } from 'redux-actions';

const doAddTodo = createAction('TODO_ADD');
```

The doAddTodo() is an action creator. It uses the specified action type 'TODO_ADD'. When using it, you can pass a payload when needed. It becomes automatically allocated under a payload property.

Code Playground

```
const action = doAddTodo({ id: '0', name: 'learn redux', completed: false });

// action: {
//   type: 'TODO_ADD',
//   payload: {
//     id: '0',
//     name: 'learn redux',
//     completed: false
//   }
// }
```

The handleAction() method is a utility for reducers. It aligns action types with reducers whereas no switch case statement is needed anymore. It takes the action type as argument and a reducer function for handling the incoming action. As third argument, it takes an initial state.

[133]https://github.com/acdlite/redux-actions

Code Playground

```
import { handleAction } from 'redux-actions';

handleAction('TODO_ADD', applyAddTodo, {});

function applyAddTodo(state, action) {
  // ...
  // return new state
}
```

The two methods `createAction()` and `handleAction()` have sibling methods for using, creating, and handling multiple actions too: `createActions()` and `handleActions()`. Especially when defining a reducer, it makes sense to map multiple action types to multiple handlers.

Code Playground

```
import { handleActions } from 'redux-actions';

const reducer = handleActions({
  TODO_ADD: applyAddTodo,
  TODO_TOGGLE: applyToggleTodo,
}, initialState);
```

As you can see, it is far more concise than defining reducers in plain JavaScript with the switch case statement.

Code Playground

```
function reducer(state = initialState, action) {
  switch(action.type) {
    case 'TODO_ADD' : {
      return applyAddTodo(state, action);
    }
    case 'TODO_TOGGLE' : {
      return applyToggleTodo(state, action);
    }
    default : return state;
  }
}
```

The drawback when using the library is that it hides how Redux works with plain JavaScript. It can be difficult for newcomers to grasp what's going on when using such utility libraries from the very beginning without understanding how actions and reducers in Redux work.

The library is only a small utility belt for Redux, yet a lot of people are using it. You can read up everything about it in the official documentation[134].

---

[134]https://github.com/acdlite/redux-actions

React Redux Libraries

Apart from the react-redux[135] library that glues together your view and state layer, there exist other libraries that can be used when you already use React and Redux. Usually, these libraries provide you with React higher-order components that are coupled to the Redux store. That way, you don't need to worry about the state management when it is shielded away from you.

For instance, when using HTML forms in React, it is often tedious to track the state of each input element in your local component. Moreover you are often confronted with validation of these forms. The library redux-form[136] helps you to keep track of the form state not in the local state but in the Redux store. It enables you to access and update the form state through a higher-order component that is connected to the Redux store. In addition, it supports you in validating your form state before a user can submit it.

Another example would be a table component in React. A plain table component in React can be easily written on your own. But what about certain features such as sorting, filtering or pagination? Then it becomes difficult, because you would have to manage the state of each initialized table component. There exist several libraries that help you to implement tables in React and glue them to the Redux store. For instance, the react-redux-composable-list[137] can be used for such cases.

There are a ton of libraries that already abstract away the state management for you when using common components such as forms or tables. Again you can have a look into this repository[138] to get to know various of these libraries. It makes sense to use battle tested abstractions as libraries before implementing them on your own.

---

[135]https://github.com/reactjs/react-redux

[136]https://github.com/erikras/redux-form

[137]https://github.com/SmallImprovements/react-redux-composable-list

[138]https://github.com/markerikson/react-redux-links

Routing with Redux

In single page applications you will introduce routing eventually. In React, there exists one preferred library for routing: React Router[139]. There should be other routing libraries for other single page application solutions. These solutions help you to navigate from URL to URL without reloading the page. That's how single page applications work after all. You only fetch your application once, but keep track of the state even when you route from URL to URL. Thus the routes in your URLs are state, too. But is it managed in the Redux store?

The common sense when using routing in Redux is that the Router handles the URL and Redux handles the state. There is no interaction between them. For instance, when you decide to store your visibility filter SHOW_ALL into your URL (domain.com?filter=SHOW_ALL) instead of your Redux store, it is fine doing it. You would only have to retrieve the state from the URL and not from the Redux store. So it depends on your own setup. In the end, the Router holds the single source of truth for the URL state and the Redux store holds the single source of truth for the application state. You can read more about this topic in the official documentation[140] of Redux.

---

[139]https://github.com/ReactTraining/react-router

[140]http://redux.js.org/docs/advanced/UsageWithReactRouter.html

Typed Redux

JavaScript by nature is an untyped language. You will often encounter bugs in your career that could have been prevented by type safety. In Redux, type safety can make a lot of sense, because you can define exactly what kind of types go into your actions, reducers or state. You could define that an action that creates a todo item would have the property name with the type String and the property completed with the type Boolean. Every time you pass a wrong typed value for these properties to create a todo item, you would get an error on compile time of your application. You wouldn't wait until your application runs to figure out that you have passed a wrong value to your action. There wouldn't be a runtime exception when you can already cover these bugs during compile time.

Typed JavaScript can be a verbose solution when working on short living or simple projects. But when working in a large code base, where code needs to be kept maintainable, it is advisable to use a type checker. It makes refactorings easier and adds a bunch of benefits to the developer experience due to editor and IDE integrations.

There exist two major solutions gradually using JavaScript as a typed language: Flow (Facebook) and TypeScript (Microsoft). While the former has its biggest impact in the React community, the latter is well adopted amongst other frameworks and libraries.

What would a type checker like Flow look like when using in Redux? For instance, in a todo reducer the state could be defined by a type:

Code Playground

```
type Todo = {
  id: string,
  name: string,
  completed: boolean,
};

type Todos = Array<Todo>;

function todoReducer(state: Todos = [], action) {
  switch(action.type) {
    case ADD_TODO : {
      return applyAddTodo(state, action);
    }
    default : return state;
  }
}
```

Now, whenever an action leads to a state that is not defined by its type definition, you would get an error on compile time of your application. In addition, you can use plugins for your editor or IDE to give you the early feedback that something is wrong with your action or reducer. As the previous example has shown type safety for reducers, you could apply the same for your action creators and selectors. Everything can be type checked. You can read more about Flow on its official site[141].

---

[141]https://flow.org/

Server-side Redux

Server-side rendering is used to render the initial page load from a server. Every further user interaction is done on the client-side. For instance, it is beneficial for SEO, because when a web crawler visits your website, it can retrieve the whole application without bothering to execute JavaScript on the client-side. It retrieves the whole application with its initial state. The initial state can already be data that is fetched from a database. In React, but also in other single page applications, there are solutions to deal with server-side rendering. However, introducing server-side rendering comes with a handful of challenges. One of these challenges is state management.

When the initial page is rendered by the server-side, the initial state must be sent as a response to the client as well. The client in return would use the initial state. For instance, imagine you want to load data from a database before you send the response from the server to the client. Somehow you would have to put this data into the response next to your server-side rendered application. Afterward, the client can use the response to render the application and would already have the initial state that comes from a database. If the data wasn't sent along in the initial server request, the client would have to fetch it again.

In Redux, you can initialize a Redux store anywhere. You can initialize it on a client-side to access and manipulate the state, but also on the server-side to provide your application with an initial state. The initial state would be put in the Redux store before the server-sided response is send to the client application. But how does it work? The Redux store on the client-side is a singleton. There is only one instance of the Redux store. On the server-side, the Redux store isn't a singleton. Every time a server-side request is made, it would initialize a new instance of the Redux store. The Redux store can be filled with an initial state before the server-side response is sent to a client.

Server-side rendering and state management open up a whole new topic. That's why the book doesn't cover the topic but only points you in the right direction. You can read more about the topic in the official Redux documentation[142].

---

[142]http://redux.js.org/docs/recipes/ServerRendering.html

MobX

The next chapters of the book will dive into an alternative library that provides a state management solution: MobX. However, the book will not allocate the same space as for Redux and thus not deeply dive into the topic. Because MobX doesn't follow an opinionated way of how to structure your state management, it is difficult to tackle it from all angles. There are several ways on where to put your state and how to update it. The book shows only a few opinionated ways, but doesn't showcase all of them.

MobX advertises itself as simple yet scalable state management library. It was created and introduced by Michel Weststrate[143] and heavily used, thus battle tested, in his own company called Mendix. MobX is an alternative to Redux for state management. It grows in popularity even though only a fraction of people uses it as a state management alternative to Redux. In a later chapter, you can read about the differences between both libraries for state management, because you may want to make an informed decision on whether you should use Redux or MobX to scale your state management.

The library uses heavily JavaScript decorators that are not widely adopted and supported by browsers yet. But they are not mandatory and you can avoid using them with plain functions instead. You can find these plain functions in the official documentation[144]. However, this book will showcase the usage of these decorators, because it is another exciting way of using JavaScript.

Along the way of the following chapters you can decide to opt-in any time the MobX + React DevTools[145]. You can install the node package with npm and follow the instructions from the GitHub repository.

---

[143]https://twitter.com/mweststrate

[144]https://mobx.js.org/

[145]https://github.com/mobxjs/mobx-react-devtools

Introduction

MobX is often used in applications that have a view layer such as React. Thus the state, similar to Redux, needs to be connected to the view. It needs to be connected in a way that the state can be updated and the updated state flows back into the view.

Concept Playground

```
View -> MobX -> View
```

The schema can be elaborated to give more detail about MobX and its parts.

Concept Playground

```
View -> (Actions) -> State -> (Computed Values) -> Reactions -> View
```

It doesn't need to be necessarily the view layer, but when using MobX in an application with components, most likely the view will either mutate the state directly or use a MobX action to mutate it. It can be as simple as a `onClick` handler in a component that triggers the mutation. However, the mutation could also be triggered by a side-effect (e.g. scheduled event).

The state in MobX isn't immutable, thus you can mutate the state directly. Actions in MobX can be used to mutate the state too, but they are not mandatory. You are allowed to mutate the state directly. There is no opinionated way around how to update the state. You have to come up with your own best practice.

In MobX the state becomes observable. Thus, when the state changes, the application reacts to the changes with so called reactions. The part of your application that uses these reactions becomes reactive. For instance, a MobX reaction can be as simple as a view layer update. The view layer in MobX becomes reactive by using reactions. It will update when the state in MobX updates.

In between of an observable MobX state and MobX reactions are computed values. These are not mandatory, similar to the MobX Actions, but add another fine-grained layer into your state. Computed values are derived properties from the state or from other computed values. Apart from the MobX state itself, they are consumed by reactions too. When using computed values, you can keep the state itself in a simple structure. Yet you can derive more complex properties from the state with computed values that are used in reactions too. Computed values evaluate lazily when used in reactions when the state changes. They don't necessarily update every time the state changes, but only when they are consumed in a reaction that updates the view.

These are basically all parts in MobX. The state can be mutated directly or by using a MobX action. Reactions observe these state changes and consume the state itself or computed values from the state or other computed values. Both ends, actions and reactions, can simply be connected to a view layer such as React. The connection can happen in a straight forward way or with a bridging library as you will experience it in the following chapters.

Observable State

The state in MobX can be everything from JavaScript primitives to complex objects, arrays or only references over to classes that encapsulate the state. Any of these properties can be made observable by MobX. When the state changes, all the reactions, for instance the reaction of the view layer, will run to re-render the view. State in MobX isn't managed in one global state object. It is managed in multiple states that are most of the time called stores or states.

Code Playground

```
const { observable } = mobx;

class TodoStore {
  @observable todos = [];
}

const todoStore = new TodoStore();
```

Keep in mind that it doesn't need to be managed in a store instance that comes from a JavaScript class. It can be a plain list of todos. The way of using stores to manage your MobX state is already opinionated. Since there are a couple of different ways on where to store your state in MobX, the book will teach the straight forward way of managing it in stores. In the end, stores enable you to manage a predictable state where every store can be kept responsible for its own substate.

The state in MobX can be mutated directly without actions:

Code Playground

```
todoStore.todos.push({ id: '0', name: 'learn redux', completed: true });
todoStore.todos.push({ id: '0', name: 'learn mobx', completed: false });
```

That means as well, that the store instances can leak into the view layer and an onClick handler could mutate the state directly in the store.

State and view layer can be coupled very closely in MobX. In comparison to Redux, it doesn't need to use explicit actions to update the state indirectly. You will get to know more about MobX actions in a later chapter.

Autorun

The autorun functionality in MobX is not often seen. It is similar to the subscription() method of the Redux store. It is always called when the observable state in MobX changes and once in the beginning when the MobX state initializes. Similar to the subscription() method of the Redux store, it is later on used to make the view layer reactive with MobX. The autorun function is only one way to produce a reaction on MobX.

However, you can use it to experiment with your state updates while learning MobX. You can simply add it to your TodoStore example.

Code Playground

```
const { observable, autorun } = mobx;

class TodoStore {
  @observable todos = [];
}

const todoStore = new TodoStore();

autorun(() => console.log(todoStore.todos.length));

todoStore.todos.push({ id: '0', name: 'learn redux', completed: true });
todoStore.todos.push({ id: '0', name: 'learn mobx', completed: false });
```

It will run the first time when the state initializes, but then every time again when the observable state updates. You can open the MobX Playground[146] to experiment with it.

Actions

As mentioned, the state can be mutated directly in MobX. But a handful of people would argue that it is a bad practice. It couples the state mutation too close to the view layer when you start to mutate the state directly in a onClick handler. Therefore, you can use MobX actions to decouple the state update and keep your state updates at one place.

Code Playground

```
const { observable, autorun, action } = mobx;

class TodoStore {
  @observable todos = [];

  @action addTodo(todo) {
    this.todos.push(todo);
  }
}
```

---

[146]https://jsbin.com/gezibazuke/1/edit?js,console

```
const todoStore = new TodoStore();

autorun(() => console.log(todoStore.todos.length));

todoStore.addTodo({ id: '0', name: 'learn redux', completed: true });
todoStore.addTodo({ id: '1', name: 'learn mobx', completed: false });
```

However, MobX is not opinionated about the way you update your state. You can use actions or mutate the state directly without an action.

Code Playground

```
class TodoStore {
  @observable todos = [];

  addTodo(todo) {
    this.todos.push(todo);
  }
}
```

In order to enforce state updates with actions, you can opt-in a configuration with the configure() functionality from MobX. There you can pass an object for global MobX confgurations whereas there is one configuration in particular to enforce actions in MobX. After you have set it to true, every state update needs to happen via an action. This way you enforce the decoupling of state mutation and view with actions.

Code Playground

```
const { observable, autorun, action, configure } = mobx;

configure({ enforceActions: true });

class TodoStore {
  @observable todos = [];

  @action addTodo(todo) {
    this.todos.push(todo);
  }
}

const todoStore = new TodoStore();
```

```
autorun(() => console.log(todoStore.todos.length));

todoStore.addTodo({ id: '0', name: 'learn redux', completed: true });
todoStore.addTodo({ id: '1', name: 'learn mobx', completed: false });
```

You can test the MobX action and the configure() function with the enforced actions in the MobX Playground[147]. In addition, it makes always sense to think thoughtfully about your actions. In the previous case, every call of addTodo() would lead all relying reactions to run. That's why the autorun function runs every time you add a todo item. So how would you accomplish to add multiple todo items at once without triggering reactions for every todo item? You could have another action that takes an array of todo items.

Code Playground

```
const { observable, autorun, action } = mobx;

class TodoStore {
  @observable todos = [];

  @action addTodo(todo) {
    this.todos.push(todo);
  }

  @action addTodos(todos) {
    todos.forEach(todo => this.addTodo(todo));
  }
}

const todoStore = new TodoStore();

autorun(() => console.log(todoStore.todos.length));

todoStore.addTodos([
  { id: '0', name: 'learn redux', completed: true },
  { id: '1', name: 'learn mobx', completed: false },
]);
```

That way, the relying reactions only evaluate once after the action got called. You can find the necessary code to play around with in the MobX Playground[148].

---

[147]https://jsbin.com/zigapodeke/1/edit?js,console
[148]https://jsbin.com/yunebovose/1/edit?js,console

Computed Values

Computed values are derived properties from the state or other computed values. They have no side-effects and thus are pure functions. The computed values help you to keep your state structure simple yet can derive complex properties from it. For instance, when you would filter a list of todos for their completed property, you could compute the values of uncompleted todo items.

Code Playground

```
const { observable, action, computed } = mobx;

class TodoStore {
  @observable todos = [];

  @action addTodo(todo) {
    this.todos.push(todo);
  }

  @computed get incompleteTodos() {
    return this.todos.filter(todo => !todo.completed);
  }
}
```

The computation happens reactively when the state has changed and a reaction asks for it. Thus, these computed values are at your disposal, apart from the state itself, for your view layer later on. In addition, they don't compute actively every time but rather only compute reactively when a reaction demands it. You can experiment with it in the MobX Playground[149].

---

[149]https://jsbin.com/tapiyuricu/1/edit?js,console

MobX in React

The basics in MobX should be clear by now. The state in MobX is mutable and can be mutated directly, by actions too or only by actions, and not directly, when enforcing actions with a configuration. When scaling your state management in MobX, you would keep it in multiple yet manageable stores to keep it maintainable. These stores can expose actions and computed values, but most important they make their properties observable. All of these facts already give you an opinionated way of how to store state (e.g. with stores) and how to update the state (e.g. explicit actions with enforced actions). However, you can decide to use a different opinionated approach.

Now, every time an observable property in a store changes, the autorun function of MobX runs. The autorun makes it possible to bridge the MobX state updates over to other environments. For instance, it can be used in a view layer, such as React, to re-render it every time the state changes. MobX and React match very well. Both libraries solve their own problem, but can be used together to build a sophisticated scaling application. The React view layer can receive the state from MobX, but also can mutate the state. It can connect to both ends: getting state and mutating it.

When you start to introduce React to your MobX Playground, you could begin to display the list of todo items from your todoStore.

Code Playground

```
class TodoList extends React.Component {
  render() {
    return (
      <div>
        {this.props.todoStore.todos.map(todo =>
          <div key={todo.id}>
            {todo.name}
          </div>
        )}
      </div>
    );
  }
}

ReactDOM.render(
  <TodoList todoStore={todoStore} />,
  document.getElementById('app')
);
```

However, when you update your MobX store nothing happens. The view layer is not notified about any state updates, because these happen outside of React. You can use the autorun function of MobX to introduce a naive re-rendering of the view layer.

Code Playground

```
function render() {
  ReactDOM.render(
    <TodoList todoStore={todoStore} />,
    document.getElementById('app')
  );
}


autorun(render);
```

Now you have one initial rendering of the view layer, because the autorun is running once initially, and successive renderings when the MobX state updates. You can play around with it in the MobX Playground[150].

There exists a neat library that bridges from MobX to React: mobx-react[151]. It spares you to use the autorun reaction in order to re-render the view layer. Instead it uses a observer decorator, that uses the autorun function under the hood, to produce a reaction. The reaction simply flushes the update to a React component to re-render it. It makes your React view layer reactive and re-renders it when the observable state in MobX has changed.

Code Playground

```
const { observer } = mobxReact;


. . .


@observer
class TodoList extends React.Component {
  render() {
    return (
      <div>
        {this.props.todoStore.todos.map(todo =>
          <div key={todo.id}>
            {todo.name}
          </div>
        )}
      </div>
```

---

[150]https://jsbin.com/delohuwidi/1/edit?js,output
[151]https://github.com/mobxjs/mobx-react

```
    );
  }
}

ReactDOM.render(
  <TodoList todoStore={todoStore} />,
  document.getElementById('app')
);
```

```
...
```

Again you can play around with it in the MobX Playground[152]. If you would want to use the TodoList component as functional component, you can use the observer as a function and not as a JavaScript decorator.

Code Playground

```
const TodoList = observer(function (props) {
  return (
    <div>
      {props.todoStore.todos.map(todo =>
        <div key={todo.id}>
          {todo.name}
        </div>
      )}
    </div>
  );
});
```

You can find the example in the following MobX Playground[153] to play around with it.

---

[152]https://jsbin.com/rusewogaza/1/edit?html,js,output
[153]https://jsbin.com/wefoyocutu/1/edit?html,js,output

Local State

As mentioned before, MobX is not opinionated about how to store your state and how to update it. It goes so far, that you can even exchange your local state in React, this.state and this.setState(), with MobX. There you wouldn't use a store which separates the state from the view, but use class properties of the component instead. The case can be demonstrated by introducing a component that adds a todo item to the list of todo items from the previous example.

Code Playground

```
ReactDOM.render(
  <div>
    <TodoAdd todoStore={todoStore} />
    <TodoList todoStore={todoStore} />
  </div>,
  document.getElementById('app')
);
```

The TodoAdd component only renders an input field to capture the name of the todo item and a button to create the todo item.

Code Playground

```
@observer
class TodoAdd extends React.Component {
  render() {
    return (
      <div>
        <input
          type="text"
          value={this.input}
          onChange={this.onChange}
        />
        <button
          type="button"
          onClick={this.onSubmit}
        >Add Todo</button>
      </div>
    );
  }
}
```

The two handlers class methods are missing. The onChange handler can be an action itself to update a internally managed value of the input field.

Code Playground

```
@observer
class TodoAdd extends React.Component {

  @observable input = '';

  onChange = (event) => {
    this.input = event.target.value;
  }

  render() {
    ...
  }
}
```

This way, the input property is not allocated in the local state of React, but in the observable state of MobX. The observer decorator makes sure that the component stays reactive to its observed properties. The onSubmit handler finally creates the todo item yet alters the local state of the component again, because it has to reset the input value and increments the identifier.

Code Playground

```
@observer
class TodoAdd extends React.Component {

  @observable input = '';
  @observable id = 0;

  onSubmit = () => {
    this.props.todoStore.addTodo({
      id: this.id,
      name: this.input,
      completed: false,
    });

    this.id++;
    this.input = '';
  }

  onChange = (event) => {
    ...
  }
```

```
render() {
    ...
  }
}
```

MobX is able to take over the local state of React. You wouldn't need to use `this.state` and `this.setState()` anymore. The previous example can be found in the MobX Playground[154]. Again you experience that MobX isn't opinionated about the way the state is managed. You can have the state management encapsulated in a store class or couple it next to a component as local state. It can make React local state obsolete. But should it? That is up to you.

---

[154]https://jsbin.com/velihicomu/2/edit?html,js,output

Scaling Reactions

Each component can be decorated with an observer to be reactive to observable state changes in MobX. When introducing a new component to display a todo item, you can decorate it as well. This TodoItem component receives the todo property, but also the todoStore in order to complete a todo item.

Code Playground

```
const TodoItem = observer(({ todo, todoStore }) => {
  return (
    <div>
      {todo.name}
      <button
        type="button"
        onClick={() => todoStore.toggleCompleted(todo)}
      >
        {todo.completed
          ? "Incomplete"
          : "Complete"
        }
      </button>
    </div>
  );
});
```

Notice that the TodoItem is a functional stateless component. In addition, in order to complete a todo item, you would have to introduce the toggleCompleted action in the TodoStore.

Code Playground

```
class TodoStore {
  @observable todos = [];

  ...

  @action toggleCompleted(todo) {
    todo.completed = !todo.completed;
  }
}
```

The TodoList component could use the TodoItem component now.

Code Playground

```
@observer
class TodoList extends React.Component {
  render() {
    return (
      <div>
        {this.props.todoStore.todos.map(todo =>
          <TodoItem
            todoStore={this.props.todoStore}
            todo={todo}
            key={todo.id}
          />
        )}
      </div>
    );
  }
};
```

In the running application you should be able to complete a todo item. The benefit of splitting up one reactive component into multiple reactive components can be seen when adding two console.log() statements.

Code Playground

```
const TodoItem = observer(({ todo, todoStore }) => {
  console.log('TodoItem: ' + todo.name);
  return (
    . . .
  );
});

@observer
class TodoList extends React.Component {
  console.log('TodoList');
  render() {
    . . .
  }
};
```

You can open up the application in the MobX Playground[155]. When you add a todo item, you will get the console.log() outputs for the TodoList component and only the newly created

---

[155]https://jsbin.com/qecawoweja/2/edit?js,console,output

TodoItem. When you complete a todo item, you will only get the `console.log()` of the completing TodoItem component. The reactive component only updates when their observable state changes. Everything else doesn't update, because the `observer` decorator implements under the hood the `shouldComponentUpdate()` lifecycle method of React to prevent the component from updating when nothing has changed. You can read more about optimizing MobX performance in React in the official documentation[156].

---

[156]https://mobx.js.org/best/react-performance.html

Inject Stores

So far, the application passes down the store from the React entry point via props to its child components. They are already passed down more than one layer. However, the store(s) could be used directly in the components by using them directly (when accessible in the file). They are only observable state. Since MobX is not opinionated about where to put state, the observable state, in this case stores, could live anywhere. But as mentioned, the book tries to give an opinionated approach as best practice.

The mobx-react[157] library provides you with two helpers to pass the observable state implicitly down to the components (via React's context) rather than passing them through every component layer explicitly.

The first helper is the `Provider` component that passes down all the necessary observable states down.

Code Playground

```
const { observer, Provider } = mobxReact;
```

```
. . .
```

You can use it in the React entry point to wrap your component tree. In addition, you can pass it any observable state that should be passed down. In this case, the observable state is the store instance.

Code Playground

```
. . .

ReactDOM.render(
  <Provider todoStore={todoStore}>
    <div>
      <TodoAdd />
      <TodoList />
    </div>
  </Provider>,
  document.getElementById('app')
);
```

However, it could be multiple stores or only a couple of observable primitives.

---

[157]https://github.com/mobxjs/mobx-react

Code Playground

```
<Provider
  storeOne={storeOne}
  storeTwo={storeTwo}
  anyOtherState={anyOtherState}
>

  ...

</Provider>
```

The second helper from the library is the `inject` decorator. You can use it for any component down your component tree that is wrapped somewhere above by the `Provider` component. It retrieves the provided observable state from React's context as props.

Code Playground

```
const { observer, inject, Provider } = mobxReact;

...

@inject('todoStore') @observer
class TodoAdd extends React.Component {

  ...

}
```

The `TodoAdd` component already has access to the `todoStore` now. You can add the injection to the other components too. It can be used as function for functional stateless components.

Code Playground

```
const TodoItem = inject('todoStore')(observer(({
  todo, todoStore
}) =>
  <div>
    {todo.name}
    <button
      type="button"
      onClick={() => todoStore.toggleCompleted(todo)}
    >
    {todo.completed
      ? "Incomplete"
      : "Complete"
    }
```

```
      </button>
    </div>
));
```

The `TodoList` component doesn't need to manually pass down the `todoStore` anymore. The `TodoItem` already accesses it via its `inject` helper.

Code Playground

```
@inject('todoStore') @observer
class TodoList extends React.Component {
  render() {
    return (
      <div>
        {this.props.todoStore.todos.map(todo =>
          <TodoItem
            todo={todo}
            key={todo.id}
          />
        )}
      </div>
    );
  }
};
```

Every component can access the observable state, that is passed to the `Provider` component, with the `inject` decorator. This way you keep a clear separation of state and view layer. You can access the project in the MobX Playground[158] again.

---

[158]https://jsbin.com/xubewezeji/3/edit?js,output

Advanced MobX

MobX is not opinionated. Thus it gives you a handful of tools to accomplish your on way of mastering state management. It would be sufficient to use the basics of MobX to introduce state management in your application. But there are more tools hidden in MobX that this chapter is going to point out. It addition, this chapter should give you a couple more pillars to understand and use MobX successfully in your own way.

Other Reactions

You have encountered two reactions by now: autorun and observer. The observer produces a reaction because it uses autorun under the hood. It is only used in the mobx-react package. Thus, both functions are used to create reactions based on observable state changes. While the autorun function can be used to re-render naively the UI, it can also used for broader domains. The observer decorator is solely used to make a view layer reactive.

However, MobX comes with more reactions. The book will not go too much into detail here, but it does no harm to be aware of other options too. The MobX when[159] is another function that produces a reaction. It is based on predicates and effects. A given predicate runs as long as it returns true. When it returns true, the effect is called. After that the autorunner is disposed. The when function returns a disposer to cancel the autorunner prematurely, so before an effect can be called.

Code Playground

```
const { observable, autorun, computed, when } = mobx;

class TodoStore {
  @observable todos = [];

  constructor() {
    when(
      // once (predicate)...
      () => this.hasCompleteTodos,
      // ... then (effect)
      () => this.celebrateAccomplishment()
    );
  }

  @computed get completeTodos() {
    return this.todos.filter(todo => todo.completed);
  }
}
```

---

[159]https://mobx.js.org/refguide/when.html

```
@computed get hasCompleteTodos() {
    return this.completeTodos.length > 0;
}

celebrateAccomplishment() {
    console.log('First todo completed, celebrate it!');
}
}

const todoStore = new TodoStore();

autorun(() => console.log(todoStore.todos.length));

todoStore.todos.push({ id: '0', name: 'finish the book', completed: false });
todoStore.todos.push({ id: '1', name: 'learn redux', completed: true });
todoStore.todos.push({ id: '2', name: 'learn mobx basics', completed: true });
todoStore.todos.push({ id: '3', name: 'learn mobx', completed: false });
```

So how many times does the reaction run? You can take your guess first and afterward open the MobX Playground[160] to experience the reaction yourself. Basically the when triggers its effect when the predicate returns true. But it only triggers once. As you can see, two todo items that are completed are added. However, the celebrateAccomplishment() method only runs once. This way MobX allows you to use its reactions to trigger side-effects. You could trigger anything ranging from an animation to an API call.

Another function in MobX, the reaction function[161] itself, can be used to produce MobX reactions too. It is a fine-grained version of autorun. Whereas autorun will always run when the observable state has changed, the reaction function only runs when a particular given observable state has changed.

Code Playground

```
const { observable, autorun, computed, reaction } = mobx;

class TodoStore {
    @observable todos = [];

    constructor() {

        reaction(
```

---

[160]https://jsbin.com/kuzadiwagi/1/edit?js,console
[161]https://mobx.js.org/refguide/reaction.html

```
    () => this.completeTodos.length,
    sizeCompleteTodos => console.log(sizeCompleteTodos + " todos completed!")
  );
}

@computed get completeTodos() {
  return this.todos.filter(todo => todo.completed);
}
}


const todoStore = new TodoStore();

autorun(() => console.log(todoStore.todos.length));

todoStore.todos.push({ id: '0', name: 'finish the book', completed: false });
todoStore.todos.push({ id: '1', name: 'learn redux', completed: true });
todoStore.todos.push({ id: '2', name: 'learn mobx basics', completed: true });
todoStore.todos.push({ id: '3', name: 'learn mobx', completed: false });
```

How many times does the reaction run? First you can have a guess, afterward you can confirm it by trying it in the MobX Playground[162].

Now you have seen two more functions in MobX that produce reactions: when and reaction. Whereas the when function only runs once an effect when the predicate returns null, the reaction runs every time when a particular observable state has changed. You can use both to trigger side-effects, such as an API call.

Be Opinionated

MobX gives you all the tools that are needed to manage state in modern JavaScript application. However, it doesn't give you an opinionated way of doing it. This way you have all the freedom to manage your state yet it can be difficult to follow best practices or to align a team on one philosophy. That's why it is important to find your own opinionated way of doing things in MobX. You have to align on one opinionated way to manage your state.

The chapters before have shown you that observable state in MobX can be far away managed in stores yet it could be used in the local state of the view layer too. Should MobX be used instead of this.state and this.setState() in React? Be clear about how close you want to keep your MobX state to your view layer.

Another thing you should have an opinion about is how you update your observable state. Do you mutate the state directly in your view? Going this path would lead to coupling your state closer to

---

[162]https://jsbin.com/jizidoyoge/1/edit?js,console

your view layer. On the other hand, you could use explicit MobX actions. It would keep your state mutation at one place. You can make them even mandatory by using the `configure()` functionality with enforced actions. That way, every state mutation would have to go through an explicit action. No direct mutations of the state would be allowed anymore. Recommendation: You should make your state mutations as explicit as possible with actions, `configure()` and the `enforceActions` flag set to true.

When using MobX to complement your view layer, you would need to decide on how to pass your state around. You can simply allocate your state next to your components, import it directly from another file using JavaScript ES6 import and export statements, pass it down explicitly (e.g. in React with props) or pass it down implicitly from your root component with `inject()` function and the `Provider` component. You should avoid to mix up these things and follow one opinionated way. Recommendation: You should use the `inject()` function and `Provider` component to make your state implicitly accessible to your view layer.

Last but not least, you would need to align on a state structure. Observable state in MobX can be anything. It can be primitives, it can be objects or arrays but it can also be store instances derived from JavaScript classes. Without mixing up everything, you would need to align on a proper state architecture. The approach to manage your state in stores, as shown in the previous chapters, gives you a maintainable way to manage your state for specific domains. In addition, you are able to keep actions, computed values and even reactions such as autorun, reaction and when in your store. Recommendation: You should use JavaScript classes to manage your state in stores. That way your state management stays maintainable by domain related stores as stakeholders.

As you can see, there are a handful of decisions to make on how to use MobX. It gives you all the freedom to decide your own way of doing things, but after all you have to establish the opinionated way yourself and stay disciplined with it.

Alternative to Redux?

After all, is MobX a viable alternative to Redux? It depends all on yourself and your requirements. Both solutions are different in their philosophy, their underlying mechanics and in their usage. Whereas Redux gives you one opinionated way of managing your state, MobX gives you only the tools to manage your state but not the way of how to do things. Redux has a large community, a vibrant ecosystem of libraries and great selection of best practices. MobX is a younger library compared to Redux, but gives you a different approach of managing your state and comes with lots of powerful features too.

The defining powers of MobX come from its reactive nature. As you have seen when you connected your view layer to MobX with observers, only the reactive components updated that relied on an observable state change. Everything else stayed untouched. In a large scale application, it can keep your view layer updates to a minimum when using MobX the right way.

In MobX you don't need to normalize your state. You can work with references and keep your state nested. It stays simple to update your state with mutations not worrying about immutability. On the other hand, you have to be cautious on how close you couple your state to your view layer. In the end, when the state is too close to your view layer, it could end up the same way as for the first generation of single page applications were two-way data binding became a mess.

If you want to read more about the differences of Redux and MobX, I recommend you to check out the following article: Redux or MobX: An attempt to dissolve the Confusion[163]. After that you might come to a more informed decision on what you want to use for state management in your own application.

---

[163]https://www.robinwieruch.de/redux-mobx-confusion/

Beyond Redux and MobX

So far, the book has taught you different approaches of state management. Whether you are using React, an alternative view layer library or a sophisticated SPA library; most of them will come with a built-in solution to deal with local state. The book has shown you React's local state management and demonstrated approaches to scale it in plain React applications. Afterward, you learned extensively about Redux as sophisticated state management library. It can be used in combination with any view layer or SPA library. The book has taught you how to use it in React applications, too. As alternative to Redux, you read about MobX as sophisticated state management library. It comes with its own advantages and disadvantages. After all, Redux and MobX give you two different approaches to opt-in sophisticated state management to your application. However, you should never forget about your local state management solution to keep your state coupled to your components rather than exposing it globally in your entire application.

What else could you use for state management in modern JavaScript applications? There is another solution that should be mentioned in the book: GraphQL. GraphQL[164] itself hasn't anything to do with state management. It is used on the server-side to expose an API with its well defined query language. When having a server application which exposes a GraphQL API instead of a RESTful API, a client application can consume it. So how does this fit into state management then? Since GraphQL has well defined constraints, there are GraphQL client libraries which a specifically designed to consume a GraphQL API. These libraries often come with their own state management implementation but also powerful features such as pagination, caching and normalization. Everything that you had to implement on your own when consuming a RESTful API, can be achieved with those GraphQL client libraries. When using such a library when having a GraphQL server, you often don't need to worry anymore about managing the state which comes from a remote API. React's local state, Redux or MobX can be used mostly for the view state only then. Everything else is managed by the GraphQL client library. So I encourage you to research these solutions when you feel confident with the learnings from this book. Checkout my courses[165] if you find something about GraphQL there.

---

[164]http://graphql.org

[165]https://roadtoreact.com

Last but not Least

Well, if I haven't lost you by now, you can read a bit further to make it to the end of this book. The last chapters of this book have the objective to inspire you to apply your learnings. You will read about further learning paths after you read the book, a life hack to improve your learning experience and other people in the React ecosystem that you might want to follow for inspirations.

So far, the book has taught you different approaches of state management. Whether you are using React, an alternative view layer library or a sophisticated SPA library; most of them will come with a built-in solution to deal with local state. The book has shown you React's local state management and demonstrated approaches to scale it in plain React applications. Afterward, you learned extensively about Redux as sophisticated state management library. It can be used in combination with any view layer or SPA library. The book has taught you how to use it in React applications, too. As alternative to Redux, you read about MobX as sophisticated state management library. It comes with its own advantages and disadvantages. After all, Redux and MobX give you two different approaches to opt-in state management to your application. However, you should never forget about your local state management solution to keep your state coupled to your components rather than exposing it in your global state.

Further Learning Paths

You have built a couple of applications in this book. While reading the chapters, you adapted the applications to apply advanced techniques, tools or features. Perhaps you even followed all of the practical chapters closely in the book. But that's not the end. It's the end of me guiding you in this learning experience, but now it's up to you to continue with it. I guess there are far more features, techniques or tools that you could apply to these applications. Be creative and challenge yourself by implementing these on your own. I am curious what you come up with, so don't hesitate to reach out to me.

The book uses React as its view layer. But React is not mandatory to utilize Redux or MobX. Other view layer libraries or even SPA frameworks have their own local state management. Yet they can be used together with Redux or MobX. You can substitute the React view layer with your own solution to build modern applications. If you haven't read the Road to learn React[166] and this book made a good job pitching React to you, you can give the other book a shot. It teaches the fundamentals of plain React by building a larger application that consumes an external REST API. Both books complement each other perfectly.

I always advocate that learning with APIs is empowering[167]. That's why I try to teach with APIs when the basics of a topic are taught. Now it's up to you to build your own applications to deepen your understanding of the tools and techniques at your disposal. For instance, you can build your own SoundCloud Client in (React and) Redux. It would consume the SoundCloud API. But there are tons of platforms out there which expose their REST APIs (Reddit, Twitter or Yelp etc.). Choose one and build a client application on top of it. I am sure, after you display some of their RESTful data, you will come up with creative features. Again, you can always reach out to me to showcase your applications. I am curious what you will build after you read the book.

Yet another challenge could be to build your own state management solution from scratch. Redux is not a large library when you inspect the source code. Your first attempt could be to duplicate its functionalities. There are several tutorials out there that already show you how to do it. But you can try it on your own, too. Perhaps you even have another concept that should be embraced by your state management library. Anyways, by building such a library yourself, you will fortify your learnings.

Redux is an open source library[168]. That's why it is possible for you to contribute to the project. It can be intimidating to contribute in open source, but it is a great return of investment. Just start by helping out for the documentation or by answering questions in GitHub issues. You will immediately find yourself in a great community of contributors. You can even go beyond it and try to solve bug issues, review pull requests or help out people on other platforms such as Reddit[169]. By contributing to the topic itself, giving back something to the community, you will grow your learnings in the topic.

---

[166]https://www.robinwieruch.de/the-road-to-learn-react/

[167]https://www.robinwieruch.de/what-is-an-api-javascript/

[168]https://github.com/reactjs/redux

[169]https://www.reddit.com/r/reactjs/

You can keep yourself educated in this area by reading articles about it. I write a lot about these topics on my personal website. You can give it a shot and dig into some of the topics. One of it gives you a list of useful tips to learn React and Redux[170]. Two more great external resources are the repositories by Mark Erikson: react-redux-links[171] and redux-ecosystem-links[172]. I would argue that you will find any solution to a problem in them. In addition, you will dive deeper into the techniques and tools in Redux.

If you want to go beyond Redux, you can give Relay Modern[173] or Apollo Client[174] a shot. Both enable you to build GraphQL[175] consuming client application. By using Relay Modern or Apollo Client, you can give your application state management in your client API layer rather than application layer. I am sure you will find more educating material on them if you search for it. In addition, I have more upcoming tutorials on those technologies if you want to keep an eye on them. Similar to the platforms that expose REST APIs, you could for instance look up platforms that expose a GraphQL API. In your own client application you could use Relay Modern to consume the API. Perhaps there already is a tutorial that explains how to consume these GraphQL APIs.

As you can see, there are endless possibilities to apply your learnings. Don't hesitate and jump into coding. I am curious what you come up with, so please reach out to me.

---

[170]https://www.robinwieruch.de/tips-to-learn-react-redux/

[171]https://github.com/markerikson/react-redux-links

[172]https://github.com/markerikson/redux-ecosystem-links

[173]https://facebook.github.io/relay/docs/relay-modern.html

[174]https://github.com/apollographql/apollo-client

[175]http://graphql.org/

Never stop Learning

I believe there is one secret when it comes to learning. There exists a principle that is called the Learning Pyramid. When you search for it in your favorite search engine, you will definitely find it. Basically, it shows the relation between retention rates and mental activities. For instance, the average student retention when doing lectures is 5%. That's not a good rate at all. Let's see how all the other mental activities break down according to their retention rates:

- **5% Lecture**
- **10% Reading** (Uuups!)
- **20% Audiovisual** (Phew... I hope you have purchased one of the greater packages to have those supplementary learnings too)
- **30% Demonstration** (Check!)
- **50% Discussion** (Did I mention that there is a Slack Group[176]?)
- **75% Practice by Doing** (Hopefully you did all the hands-on parts of this books on your own! If you have purchased the Source Code as well, use these to internalize your learnings.)
- **90% Teach Others** (Join the Slack Group[177] to mentor other developers learning about React and its ecosystem!)

Perhaps you recall it from somewhere, but it is always refreshing to see it again. In the beginning of the book, I told you that nobody became perfect by reading a book. You have to apply your learnings. I hope that I arranged the book in a way, enabling you with all the techniques and exercises along the way, that you can learn form these experiences. In addition, I gave you some more learning paths to practice by doing in the last chapter.

Finally, let's get to the one secret about learning that I mentioned. It is the bottom item in the pyramid that has the biggest return of investment: Teaching. Personally, I made the same experience when I started to write about my experiences in web development on my website, answered questions on Quora[178], Reddit and Stack Overflow, and wrote a book(s). You have to dive deep into a topic in order to teach it to others. You learn about the little nuances and you dive deep into these topics because you want to teach them the right way. It's not a shallow learning experience, because you get to know every detail in order to explain it precisely. You will learn tons of stuff that you didn't know before. And most importantly, you will internalize these things by teaching it to others.

After all, you can't know everything. No one is an expert in everything. I challenge myself too, by trying to teach others about web development. I get great feedback from people, positive and negative, that I can apply to grow myself. You can do it as well. You can become better by challenging yourself, teach something to others and grow.

---

[176]https://slack-the-road-to-learn-react.wieruch.com/
[177]https://slack-the-road-to-learn-react.wieruch.com/
[178]https://www.quora.com/profile/Robin-Wieruch

So here is my quest for you after you read this book. I am sure that you have a friend, coworker or perhaps someone you know only online, from Stack Overflow or Reddit, who is keen to learn about the topics taught in this book. Schedule a get-together with this person and teach him/her about it. You can take this book as guidance. After all, teaching others is a win-win situation. Both participants, mentor and student, will grow from it. So my advice for you: Become a mentor, teach others and grow.

Acknowledgements

Foremost, I want to acknowledge the work of the people who provide us with the solutions to build modern applications nowadays. The true heroes are the people behind the tools we use every day in software development. And these solutions are mostly built in the free time of these people. Just give yourself one minute and think about all the libraries you use in your own applications.

I want to thank Dan Abramov[179] and Andrew Clark[180] for open sourcing Redux. A whole community has gathered behind this library and I must admit that it's a great community. In addition, I'd like to thank Michel Weststrate[181] for providing an alternative. It keeps the whole ecosystem in balance if there is more than one solution. These solutions can learn from each other or provide different approaches to one problem. But it always helps to think out of the box and solve problems from different perspectives.

Again, I want to thank Dan Abramov for guiding a whole generation of JavaScript developers. You work on solutions, such as create-react-app, that make a developer's life easier when getting started in React. You work closely with the community, listening to their pains and provide solutions for those problems. Moreover, you encourage people to contribute in the ecosystem. Each day, there are more contributors for react[182], create-react-app[183] and redux[184]. You give people a platform to share their knowledge. For instance, that's how you encouraged me to write about my experiences working with React and Redux. Without you sharing the content people are writing, often it would never reach a broader audience. You drive people to come up with things that other people could use to solve their problems. The book wouldn't have happened without Dan sharing my content over the last year.

I want to thank Mark Erikson[185] for his perpetual desire to help others in the world of React and Redux. He is the keeper of the great lists (react-redux-links[186]) and (redux-ecosystem-links[187]) that you definitely need to check out. There is not a day passing by that I wouldn't see a helpful comment of Mark on Reddit or Twitter about React or Redux. In addition, he is one of the many contributors in open source who shape the libraries to become a great place for newcomers.

I want to thank Christopher Chedeau[188] for his talk at React Europe 2016[189] about being successful in open source. It had a lasting impact on me and was at the time when I published my first blog post. Thank you for your work with the community.

I want to thank my people at Small Improvements who are great mentors and always a true source

---

[179] https://twitter.com/dan_abramov

[180] https://twitter.com/acdlite

[181] https://twitter.com/mweststrate

[182] https://github.com/facebook/react

[183] https://github.com/facebookincubator/create-react-app

[184] https://github.com/reactjs/redux

[185] https://twitter.com/acemarke

[186] https://github.com/markerikson/react-redux-links

[187] https://github.com/markerikson/redux-ecosystem-links

[188] https://twitter.com/Vjeux

[189] https://www.youtube.com/watch?v=nRF0OVQL9Nw

of inspiration. They supported me to make the leap educating others about the things I do in my daily work. If you ever wanted to work at a company with a great working culture, you should definitely consider Small Improvements[190]. I will always remember a coworker saying: *"It doesn't feel like work. Every day it is like coming to a place to work with friends on a great project."*

I want to thank Per Fragemann, CEO of Small Improvements, for the chance to work, taking responsibilities and grow at Small Improvements. He sees opportunities in people, believes in a sustainable company culture, and gives people all they need to strive. His values taught me a lot.

A special thanks goes to Charisse Ysabel de Torres[191] who contributed the awesome cover for the book in her free time. She was keen to help me with it and in a few brainstorm and several sketching sessions, she came up with an amazing illustration. I couldn't have done it without you. Thank you for being a source of inspiration, a great coworker and friend at Small Improvements.

In the end, I want to thank my girlfriend Liesa[192] for always being supportive. Writing a book can be an enduring battle. There were several weekends, mornings and evenings where I just sat down to write this book. She prevented me from getting into burnout and managed a lot in my life. Now, after the book is written, I hope we can have a few more relaxed weekends again. Liesa is doing most of my marketing efforts. I wouldn't be able to these things on my own as a software engineer. So if you are looking for someone to advertise your stuff, reach out to her!

Last but not least, I want to thank the React community. It's a highly creative and innovative yet friendly place that makes it possible for everyone to build effortless applications. The community is supportive and welcoming to everyone. It provides every newcomer with useful resources to get started. I hope I can contribute to this community as well by writing about these things. One of my objective is to broaden the diversity among developers by providing free learning material to minorities. Reach out to me, if you are from an underrepresented group, to get a free copy of this book.

Thank you.

---

[190]https://www.small-improvements.com/

[191]https://dribbble.com/charisseysabel

[192]https://www.iamliesa.com/

Thank You

Foremost, I want to thank you for reading the book or taking the full blown course. My biggest hope is that you had a great learning experience with the material. You should feel empowered now to build your own applications with the learned tools and techniques. Reach out to me, if you have any kind of feedback. I strive to go more in the direction of education which is why I depend on your feedback.

You can visit my website[193] to find more topics about software engineering, web development and personal growth. If you like to get any updates from me, you can subscribe to my Newsletter[194]. The updates will only be quality content and never spam. In addition, I recommend to read again the further learning paths from one of the recent chapters. Otherwise, grab a friend of yours or join the Slack Group to teach others about your learnings from the book.

In the end, if you liked the learning experience, I hope you will recommend the book to other people. Just think about people in your life who want to learn more about these topics which are taught in this book. I believe you will find someone who appreciates to learn with this book and with your help as a mentor.

Thank you for reading the book. Robin

---

[193]https://www.robinwieruch.de
[194]https://www.getrevue.co/profile/rwieruch

Copyright

CPSIA information can be obtained
at www.ICGtesting.com
Printed in the USA
LVHW102059190420
654029LV00008B/464